Resurrecting
the Book of Mormon

65 Days of Miracles

Marilynne Todd Linford

Art by Richard W. Linford

Prelude

In 2015, my first book on the Book of Mormon, *The Book of Mormon Is True: Evidences and Insights to Strengthen Your Testimony*, showed up on bookstore shelves. Until recently, I never considered there would be a second. But then I broke ten vertebrae, necessitating three surgeries, and have been homebound for almost two years. In that unwelcome state, my Relief Society president, with the bishop's approval, asked me to teach a weekly Zoom class on the Book of Mormon. With abundant heavenly and earthly help, I've been able to teach it. To my surprise, while researching for the class, I found evidences I hadn't included in my first book, or if they are included, additional information has come to my attention. While my first book focused on technical aspects, this book—*Resurrecting the Book of Mormon: 65 Days of Miracles*—centers on concepts, doctrines, and witnesses.

I thank my daughter, Elizabeth Lehnhof, who did the content edit; Shonna Linford, my daughter-in-law, who did the grammatical edit; and Stacey Turner, who did everything else, including getting it ready for publication. I appreciate their patience and skills. I thank my dear husband, Richard, who has been my caregiver and motivation during the long ordeals of healing, preparing weekly classes, and writing this book. I couldn't have done it without him.

I hope the following pages will be a measure of my gratitude for the Book of Mormon and of my testimony of the gospel of Jesus Christ.

Contents

Explaining the Title

THE GOLD PLATES WERE BURIED in a stone box in the ground and brought forth miraculously as though out of a tomb, resurrected as Jesus Christ was. The Book of Mormon: Another Testament of Jesus Christ is a living witness of Him.

My husband introduced this connection between resurrection and the gold plates by showing me his painting of the plates in the box still in the ground. He asked what I thought of it. I told him I liked it but I didn't know what was in the lefthand corner of the box. He said, "It's the stone like the stone rolled away from the tomb at Jesus' Resurrection." I must have looked puzzled because he continued, "Joseph said, 'Having removed the earth, I obtained a lever, which I got fixed under the edge of the stone, and with a little exertion raised it up' (Joseph Smith—History 1:52). The Book of Mormon has been resurrected from its tomb." "That's profound!" I said. "The living gospel of Jesus Christ has been brought forth from the grave as the Book of Mormon!"

The title cites 65 days because that is how long it took Joseph Smith, Oliver Cowdery, and other scribes, to translate almost all of the Book of Mormon. They worked on the manuscript from April 7 to June 30, 1829. If you subtract travel time and time attending to the basic duties of life, what remains is sixty-five days or less. "Conservatively estimated, this leaves sixty-five or fewer working days on which the Prophet and his scribes could have translated. That works out to be an average of eight pages per day. At such a pace, only about a week could have been taken to translate all of 1 Nephi; a day and a half for King Benjamin's speech. Considering the complexity, consistency, clarity, artistry, accuracy, density, and profundity of the Book of Mormon, the Prophet Joseph's translation is a phenomenal feat" (https://www.churchofjesuschrist.org/study/ensign/1988/01/i-have-a-question/how-long-did-it-take-joseph-smith-to-translate-the-book-of-mormon?lang=eng).

Yes! "A phenomenal feat!" The Book of Mormon is a miracle, another resurrection.

Setting the Stage

Let's set the stage for the commencement of sixty-five days of miracles. Joseph and Emma Smith are living in a small home near Emma's parents in Harmony, Pennsylvania. June 1828 is a month of loss for Joseph and Emma. They bury their first infant, a son, and the 116 manuscript pages go missing. The losses continue when Moroni takes from Joseph the interpreters, and the Lord chastises Joseph: "How oft you have transgressed the commandments and the laws of God, and have gone on in the persuasions of men. . . . You should not have feared man more than God. . . . You should have been faithful; and he would have extended his arm and supported you against all the fiery darts of the adversary; and he would have been with you in every time of trouble. . . . And this is the reason that thou hast lost thy privileges for a season" (D&C 3:6–8, 14). Joseph suffers and repents. The Urim and Thummim are returned on September 22 (Lucy Mack Smith, *The Revised and Enhanced History of Joseph Smith by His Mother*, ed. Scot Facer Proctor and Maurine Jensen Proctor [Salt Lake City: Deseret Book, 1996], 176).

Time passes. In March 1829, Joseph receives two instructions from the Lord: translate "a few more pages," which he does with Emma and Martin Harris as scribes, and then "stop for a season" (D&C 5:30). The work on the gold plates is at a standstill.

On April 5, 1829, near sunset, Joseph's younger brother Samuel Smith and Oliver Cowdery arrive at Joseph and Emma's home. They have walked 150 miles from Palmyra, New York. The visit is more than social. Samuel has come to help with the farm, so Joseph can spend his time doing the Lord's work, and Oliver wants to help Joseph.

Oliver had learned about Joseph's visions while boarding with Joseph Sr. and Lucy Mack Smith in Palmyra. At first, Joseph Sr. and Lucy were reluctant to share details of Joseph's visions with Oliver because of intense local persecution; then gradually, he gained their trust. Oliver's enthusiasm was undeniable: "The subject upon which we were yesterday conversing seems working in my very bones, and I cannot, for a moment, get it out of my mind; finally, I have resolved on what I will do. Samuel, I understand, is going down to Pennsylvania to spend the spring with Joseph; I shall make my arrangements to be ready to accompany him thither, . . . for I have made it a subject of prayer, and I firmly believe that it is the will of the Lord that I should go. If there is a work for me to do in this thing, I am determined to attend to it" (*History of Joseph Smith,* 139). Oliver confided to Joseph that the "Lord unto appeared to [him] and shewed unto him the plates" (https://www.josephsmithpapers.org/paper-summary/history-circa-summer-1832/6).

Two days later, Joseph begins dictating, and Oliver begins scribing. This process is referred to as a *translation,* but Joseph didn't translate in the typical way someone translates—from one language to another. He didn't learn Reformed Egyptian, the language of the Book of Mormon. Rather, he *dictated* by the "mercy of God, by the power of God" (D&C 1:29). He read words as they appeared in English on the Urim and Thummim (seer stone) and spoke them out loud to a scribe. This means when you read the first words in the Book of Mormon, "I, Nephi, having been born of goodly parents" (1 Nephi 1:1), you are reading the translated words Nephi spoke over 2,600 years ago!

Resurrecting the Book of Mormon is a book of twenty-two evidences that the Book of Mormon could not have been completed in sixty-five working days without moment-by-moment miracles. This sacred book of scripture truly is "a marvelous work and a wonder" (2 Nephi 25:17). No one could have created the intricate detail, the counterpointed storylines with flash forwards and flashbacks, the consistent doctrine, the hundreds of place and people names, the unique vocabularies, the hundreds of prophecies, and so much more without years of research, planning, and genius, yet there they are. The Book of Mormon is a masterpiece that has withstood constant unfriendly, even vile, scrutiny for almost two hundred years. However, these twenty-two tangible evidences are twenty-two more than you need in order to know the Book of Mormon is true. The pivotal witness comes from the Holy Ghost when you ask God in prayer.

That is the Book of Mormon promise. When you read it with sincerity and "ask God, the Eternal Father, in the name of Christ, if these things are not true . . . he will manifest the truth of it unto you, by the power of the Holy Ghost" (Moroni 10:4). I present these evidences to you with my love and thanksgiving for the Book of Mormon: Another Testament of Jesus Christ.

Evidence 1
More Names of Jesus Christ

IN ASSEMBLING EVIDENCES OF THE Book of Mormon, I decided the most important goal is to verify the Book of Mormon as "Another Testament of Jesus Christ," the subtitle added in 1982. This revelatory change states the purpose of the book and invites readers to learn more about Him and from Him. As the prophet Nephi wrote: "We talk of Christ, we rejoice in Christ, we preach of Christ, we prophesy of Christ, and we write according to our prophecies, that our children may know to what source they may look for a remission of their sins" (2 Nephi 25:26). The subtitle puts His name on the cover as evidence of His centrality to the Church that bears His name: The Church of Jesus Christ of Latter-day Saints.

A few years ago, I typed the Book of Mormon. Every time I found one of Jesus Christ's names, I put it on a spreadsheet. By the time I was finished, there were seventy-two names on the list. The more I study them, the clearer it becomes that these seventy-two names of Christ were not used randomly or for variety. The ancient writers of the Book of Mormon used specific names for Christ to fit the circumstances about which they were writing.

Many of the seventy-two names have metaphoric or symbolic meanings. For example, *Redeemer* has to do with the economy of heaven. He redeemed, or paid, for us. The word *Savior* means He rescues. Other names define Christ's relationship to God the Father—Son, Beloved Son, Son of the Eternal Father. *Lamb* and *Lamb of God* represent sacrifice and Christ's humility and obedience to His Father. Many names are words of power and authority: Lord of the Vineyard, Lord of Hosts, Mighty God, Mighty One of Israel, Most High God, King, Lord God Almighty.

In studying Christ's names throughout scripture, I have noticed that certain prophets prefer certain names. Nephi uses *Lamb of God* 32 of the 38 times it is found in all scripture. This is not unusual. Job uses *Almighty* 32 times, two-thirds of its total usage in the Old Testament. In the New Testament, the Apostle Paul uses *Christ Jesus* almost exclusively. When I was memorizing "The Living Christ," I made note of the exact way His roles and names create a visual image to testify of Him.

I discovered 12 of His 72 names are unique to the Book of Mormon, which means the Book of Mormon prophets understood Jesus Christ and His mission with additional clarity. It is possible these names were found on the brass plates. (The number following each name shows how many times that name is found in the Book of Mormon.)

Being (5)	Lord Omnipotent (4)
Beloved (2)	Man (1)
Eternal Head (1)	One (1)
Eternal Judge (1)	Savior Jesus Christ (2)
Holy God (2)	Son of Righteousness (3)
Holy Messiah (2)	Well Beloved (1)

Four examples from this list will show the uniqueness of each name and how that name fits the situation purposefully.

"Man." Of the 3,453 times *man* is found in scripture, as far as I know, it is capitalized only one time, in 3 Nephi 11:8.

"Son of Righteousness" is only found 3 times in all of scripture, all in the Book of Mormon. It is separated by hundreds of pages and hundreds of years but uses similar words to show *Son of Righteousness* means healer and giver of peace.

- "The Son of Righteousness shall appear unto them; and he shall *heal* them, and they shall have *peace* with him" (2 Nephi 26:9; emphasis added).
- The Lord said: "But unto you that fear my name, shall the Son of Righteousness arise with *healing* in his wings" (3 Nephi 25:2; emphasis added).
- Emer "lived four [more] years, and he saw *peace* in the land; yea, and he even saw the Son of Righteousness, and did rejoice and glory in his day; and he died in peace" (Ether 9:22; emphasis added).

"Being" is found 617 times throughout scripture. Only 5 of those are capitalized—all in the Book of Mormon. Like *Lord* and *God*, however, it is impossible to tell if these uses of *Being* refer to our Heavenly Father or to Jesus Christ. In context I looked for what *Being* meant to the Book of Mormon writers who used it. I was happy to see four adjacent words: *supreme, merciful, holy, unchangeable.*

"Lord Omnipotent" is found 4 times in all scripture, all in the Book of Mormon, clustered in Mosiah chapters 3–5. King Benjamin prophesies that the time is not far distant when the Lord Omnipotent will come to earth and that there is no other name whereby salvation comes. King Benjamin defines *Lord Omnipotent* as He "who reigneth, who was, and is from all eternity to all eternity" (Mosiah 3:5). The word "reign" is a regal word meaning *King*, or *all-powerful Lord.* When King Benjamin finishes speaking, he asks the people if they believe his words, and they answer: "We know of their surety and truth, because of the Spirit of the *Lord Omnipotent*, which has wrought a mighty change in us" (Mosiah 5:2; emphasis added). The people's hearts were changed by the power of His omnipotence.

Songwriter Michael McLean wrote a song called "The Man with Many Names." Knowledge about this Man with many names increases as we study His names in the Book of Mormon. I marvel at the consistency and power with which His names are used. I enjoy reading the list out loud; I feel the Spirit when I do. Like Nephi using "Lamb of God," Job using "Almighty," and Paul using "Christ Jesus," is there a name that especially resonates with you? If so, take time to find the definition and study it. The names of Christ are distributed throughout the Book of Mormon to teach and edify.

The 72 Names of Jesus Christ Found in the Book of Mormon

Almighty (2); Almighty God (3); Alpha and Omega (1)

Being (5); Beloved (2); Beloved Son (3)

Christ (308); Christ Jesus (1); Christ the Son (1); Christ the Son of God (3); Christ the Son of the Living God (3); Counselor (1); Creator (9)

Eternal God (7); Eternal Head (1); Eternal Judge (1); Everlasting Father (1)

Father (14)

God (1,676); God of Abraham (5); the God of Abraham, [and] the God of Isaac, [and] the God of Jacob (5); God of Israel (11); God of Jacob (6)

Holy Child (1); Holy God (2); Holy Messiah (2); Holy One (8); Holy One of Jacob (2)

Immanuel (2)

Jehovah (2); Jesus (117); Jesus Christ (35); Jesus Christ the Son of God (11)

King (3)

Lamb (35); Lamb of God (35); Lord (1,565); Lord God (104); Lord God Almighty (4); Lord God Omnipotent (2); Lord God of Hosts (5); Lord

Jehovah (1); Lord Jesus (1); Lord Jesus Christ (14); Lord of Hosts (52); Lord of the Vineyard (33, all in Jacob 5); Lord Omnipotent (4); Lord their God (65)

Maker (4); Man (1); Mediator (2); Messiah (32); Mighty God (2); Mighty One of Israel (1); Mighty One of Jacob (2); Most High (1); Most High God (4)

Only Begotten of the Father (4); Only Begotten Son (5)

Prince of Peace (1)

Redeemer (40); Redeemer of Israel (1)

Savior (10); Savior Jesus Christ (2); Son (43); Son of God (51); Son of Righteousness (3); Son of the Eternal Father (2); Supreme Being (1); Supreme Creator (1)

Well Beloved (1); Wonderful (1).

Note: For this list, I only counted His names that are capitalized. One example, "good shepherd" is not capitalized in the Bible or in the Book of Mormon, so I didn't count it as a name. Also, I was unsure how to count *Lord,* *God,* and other names that could apply to Heavenly Father or Jesus Christ, so I used the complete number in the tabulation.

This miracle and more in 65 working days.

Evidence 2
Premier Doctrine Restored

BOTH THE BIBLE AND THE Book of Mormon contain the gospel of Jesus Christ. However, over time, many core doctrines and principles were lost, altered, or removed from the Bible. An angel revealed to Nephi: "They have taken away from the gospel of the Lamb many parts which are plain and most precious," and because of the loss of these teachings, "an exceedingly great many do stumble, yea, insomuch that Satan hath great power over them" (1 Nephi 13:26, 29). Happily, the angel prophesied that these truths would be restored: "These last records [the Book of Mormon] shall make known the plain and precious things which have been taken away from [the Bible]" (1 Nephi 13:40).

One of the greatest truths lost to the world is the plan of salvation, our premier doctrine. It is not mentioned by name in the Bible. I believe it was deliberately removed because the word *plan* is not found in the Bible. The *concepts* of the plan of salvation can be found in the Bible, but you have to know what you are looking for; they are veiled and seemingly unrelated. You can find the Biblical references that teach the plan of salvation in *The Encyclopedia of Mormonism*, "The Plan of Salvation," Macmillan Company, New York City, New York, 1992, 1088–1091.

While the plan has been veiled in the Old and New Testaments, the good news is that it has been restored and reverberates anew in the pages of the Book of Mormon. The word *plan* is found 43 times in the Book of Mormon, 2 times in the Doctrine and Covenants, and 2 times in the Pearl of Great Price. Every time *plan* is used, it references the plan of our Father in Heaven. The plan encompasses all of eternity—past, present, and future, the magnitude of which is beyond our ability to fully appreciate at this point in our eternal progression. This divine plan has six names:

- "The great and eternal plan of deliverance" (2 Nephi 11:5)

- "The plan of restoration" (Alma 41:2)
- "The great plan of redemption" (Jacob 6:8 and 5 times in Alma. In Alma 34:16, it is called "the great and eternal plan of redemption." "Plan of redemption is found 9 more times in Alma.)
- "The plan of mercy" (Alma 42:15, "great plan of mercy" Alma 42:31)
- "The plan of salvation" (Jarom 1:2, Alma 24:14, Alma 42:5)
- "The plan of happiness" (Alma 42:16).

Each of these six names describes Jesus Christ. He is our Deliverer, our Restorer, our Redeemer, our Mercy, our Savior, and our Happiness. In April 2022, President Dallin H. Oaks added another name. He said it is the "loving plan" of a "loving Father in Heaven" (https://www.churchofjesuschrist.org/study/general-conference/2022/04/51oaks?lang=eng). President Oaks makes the point that the Father's plan is fulfilled, or we could say *activated,* by His Beloved Son.

The Father's plan is the gospel of Jesus Christ. It encompasses the Creation, the Fall, and the Atonement of Jesus Christ. It includes the gift of agency, the opportunity and blessing to choose which commandments to obey and which covenants to make and keep. Children of God, all humankind, are tested by opposites and opposition. Evil is a reality, and each of us is tempted to stray from the covenant path. All of us sin and "come short of the glory of God" (Romans 3:23). When we choose evil or fall short, we can repent because of the Atonement of Jesus Christ. Knowledge of the plan of salvation provides hope and motivation to make good choices so we can live forever as families in Heavenly Father's presence.

Both Nephi and Jacob testify of this overarching plan. Nephi said: "My soul delighteth in the covenants of the Lord which he hath made to our fathers; yea, my soul delighteth in his grace, and in his justice, and power, and mercy in the great and eternal plan of deliverance from death" (2 Nephi 11:5). Nephi's brother Jacob echoed these words with enthusiasm: "O how great the plan of our God" (2 Nephi 9:13). We also exclaimed with enthusiasm in the premortal sphere when the plan was explained to us. We "shouted for joy" (Job 38:7).

Heavenly Father wants us to know His plan. He revealed elements of it to Lehi in his well-known vision of the tree of life. Lehi finds himself in a "dark and dreary wilderness." After traveling for "the space of many hours," he prays for mercy. He sees a "large and spacious field" where there is "a tree, whose fruit was desirable to make one happy." When he arrives at the tree, he falls down in recognition that the tree of life is Jesus Christ. He partakes of the fruit and is filled with "exceedingly great joy." He wants his family to partake of the fruit (1 Nephi 8:4–12).

In the plan of salvation, we are sent away from our heavenly home to a dark and dreary wilderness called Earth. We wander, feel alone, get lost, and at some point, pray for guidance. We find the tree and partake of the fruit of the gospel. It fills us with exceedingly great joy. We desire our families to partake. This is the happy message missionaries carry to the far corners of the earth and that members of the Church share with their neighbors.

The plan of happiness is elevating, exquisite, expansive, encouraging, all-encompassing, and eternal. How blessed we are that the Book of Mormon restored this foundational doctrine, illuminating the way to return to the Father.

All this and more in 65 days.

Evidence 3
Urim and Thummim

THE WORD *URIM* AND/OR THE phrase *Urim and Thummim* are used seven times in scripture. In Old Testament times, the priest "put the breastplate upon him: also he put in the breastplate the Urim and the Thummim" (Leviticus 8:8).

In Hebrew, *Urim* and *Thummim* means "Lights and Perfections" (https://www.churchofjesuschrist.org/study/scriptures/bd/urim-and-thummim?lang=eng). Apostle Orson Pratt added this to the definition: "The Urim and Thummim is a stone or other substance sanctified and illuminated by the Spirit of the living God, and presented to those who are blessed with the gift of seeing" (*Masterful Discourses of Orson Pratt*, 552). A person who has the "gift of seeing" is called a seer. We sustain the fifteen latter-day Apostles as "prophets, seers, and revelators." G. Homer Durham (1911–1985), a General Authority, clarified: "A prophet is a teacher of known truth; a seer is a perceiver of hidden truth, a revelator is a bearer of new truth" (*Evidences and Reconciliations,* arr. G. Homer Durham, 3 vols. in 1 [1960], 257–258).

In the Book of Mormon, we learn that the brother of Jared and Mosiah used a Urim and Thummim. And more recently, Joseph Smith received a Urim and Thummim in a stone box with the gold plates. When Joseph told his mother about the items in the box, Lucy became exceedingly anxious. She wrote,

> *I trembled so with fear, lest all might be lost in consequence of some*
> *failure in keeping the commandments of God, that I was under*
> *the necessity of leaving the room in order to conceal my feelings.*
> *Joseph saw this, and said, "Do not be uneasy mother, all is right—*
> *see here, I have got a key." I knew not what he meant, but took the*
> *article of which he spoke into my hands, and, upon examination,*
> *found that it consisted of two smooth three-cornered diamonds*
> *set in glass, and the glasses were set in silver bows, which were*

connected with each other in much the same way as old fashioned
spectacles. He took them again and left me, but said nothing
respecting the Record (https://witnessesofthebookofmormon.org/
other-witnesses/lucy-mack-smith).

Lucy also wrote about seeing the breastplate. "On the morning of September 22, after Joseph had returned from the hill, "He handed me the breastplate spoken of in his history. It was wrapped in a thin muslin handkerchief; so thin that I could feel its proportions without any difficulty: It was concave on one side and convex on the other; and extended from the neck downwards as far as the center of the stomach of *a man of extraordinary size*. It had four straps of the same material for the purpose of fastening it to the breast" (https://www.josephsmithpapers.org/paper-summary/lucy-mack-smith-history-1845/121, emphasis added).

You saw the phrase "a man of extraordinary size" in Lucy's quote above. Who was this man of extraordinary size? It was the brother of Jared who used this same breastplate and Urim and Thummim. How do we know this? The Lord speaking to the men who would become the Three Witnesses said: "Behold, I say unto you, that you must rely upon my word, which if you do with full purpose of heart, you shall have a view of the plates, and also of the breastplate, the sword of Laban, the Urim and Thummim, which were given to the brother of Jared upon the mount, when he talked with the Lord face to face" (Doctrine and Covenants 17:1).

Joseph described his experience of using the Urim and Thummim (seer stone) as "the gift and power of God" (title page of the Book of Mormon), and there is precedent for a divine instrument with writing on it communicating God's will. Nephi wrote about the Liahona: "And there was also written upon them a new writing, which was plain to be read, which did give us understanding concerning the ways of the Lord; and it was written and changed from time to time, according to the faith and diligence which we gave unto it" (1 Nephi 16:29).

Joseph had more to learn about the history of the Urim and Thummim, as he was dictating to Oliver. One day he read, while using the Urim and Thummim: "And now he translated them by the means of those two stones which were fastened into the two rims of a bow. Now these things were prepared from the beginning, and were handed down from generation to generation, for the purpose of interpreting languages; and they have been kept and preserved by the hand of the Lord, that he should discover to every creature who should possess the land the iniquities and abominations of his people; and whosoever has these things is called seer, after the manner of old times" (Mosiah 28:13–16). Can you imagine translating with the Urim and Thummim and reading about Mosiah, another prophet, translating by the Urim and Thummim? I don't know how Joseph felt, but I would have felt a camaraderie with Mosiah and been amazed that another prophet had done this before!

Our knowledge of the Urim and Thummim illustrates a truth about the gospel of Jesus Christ that is repeated throughout scripture. The Apostle Paul wrote: "Jesus Christ [is] the same yesterday, and to day, and for ever" (Hebrews 13:8), meaning the work of the Father stays consistent past, present, and future. Moroni testified to the same truth: "And I would exhort you, my beloved brethren, that ye remember that he is the same yesterday, today, and forever" (Moroni 10:19).

Because God is unchanging, prophets in the *present* will have access to a Urim and Thummim, according to God's wisdom and timing. Doctrine and Covenants 130:8-11 explains that God resides on a great Urim and Thummim, that the earth when it is sanctified will be a Urim and Thummim to its inhabitants, and that from the Urim and Thummim all things pertaining to an inferior kingdom, or all kingdoms of a lower order, will be manifest to those who dwell on it. In addition we learn, that "a white stone is given to each of those who come into the celestial kingdom, whereon is a new name written, which no man knoweth save he that receiveth it. The new name is the key word."

All this and more in 65 working days.

Evidence 4
Consistent Doctrine

CRITICS OF THE BOOK OF Mormon seldom speak of the doctrine found between the covers. Neglecting the consistent doctrine of Christ through 531 pages, 11 engravers, words of 57 authors, 1,000 years of history plus the Jaredite nation's timeline is like eating the cardboard instead of the pizza. Naysayers speak of unknowns such as onties, cureloms, and adieu, which all have good answers, by the way. By focusing on minute issues, they attempt to divert attention from the core. The consistency and abundance of doctrine is very strong evidence of its authenticity. There is no other explanation of how this could happen except that the Book of Mormon is of ancient origin and came to the world just as the Prophet Joseph Smith said.

The doctrine of Jesus Christ remains coherent and constant, as taught by prophet after prophet throughout the Book of Mormon. To illustrate this fact, I researched the following nine topics: *baptism, covenant, Holy Ghost, mercy, resurrection, prophet, hope, faith,* and *repentance.* Judge for yourself how anyone could dictate such a broad, solid, unyielding doctrinal treatise without notes, drafts, years of research, planning, organizing, composing, editing, or revising with a team of skilled assistants in sixty-five working days. The power of each word bears testimony over and over again to the strength of this evidence.

Baptize (all forms of the word) is found cover to cover—1 Nephi to Moroni—145 times:

1 Nephi 10:9–10; 1 Nephi 11:27; 1 Nephi 20:1; 2 Nephi 9:23–24; 2 Nephi 31:4–6, 8, 11–14, 17; Mosiah 18:3, 10, 13, 15–18, 21, 35; Mosiah 21:33, 35; Mosiah 25:17–18, Mosiah 26:4, 15, 22, 37; Alma 4:4–5; Alma 5:3, 62; Alma 6:2; Alma 7:14–15; Alma 8:5, 10; Alma 9:27; Alma

15:12–14; Alma 19:35; Alma 32:16; Alma 48:19; Alma 49:30; Alma 62:45; Helaman 3:24, 26; Helaman 5:17, 19; Helaman 16:1, 3–5; 3 Nephi 1:23; 3 Nephi 7:24–26; 3 Nephi 9:20; 3 Nephi 11:21–23, 25, 27–28, 33–34, 37–38; 3 Nephi 12:1–2; 3 Nephi 18:5, 11, 16, 30; 3 Nephi 19:11–13; 3 Nephi 21:6; 3 Nephi 23:5; 3 Nephi 26:17, 21; 3 Nephi 27:1, 16, 20; 3 Nephi 28:18; 3 Nephi 30:2; 4 Nephi 1:1; Mormon 3:2; Mormon 7:8, 10; Mormon 9:23, 29; Ether 4:18; Ether 12:14; Moroni 7:34; Moroni 6:1–5, 10–15, 20, 22, 25; Moroni 7:34; Moroni 8:5, 9–15, 20, 22, 25.

A Book of Mormon thought about baptism:
The common question "Since Jesus was holy, why did He need to be baptized?" has a common answer: "To fulfill all righteousness." However, that only describes the role of the Son of God. As mortals, *we* are not baptized to fulfill all righteousness. There is an answer as to why Jesus was baptized, however, that applies to everyone: "Notwithstanding he being holy, he showeth unto the children of men that, according to the flesh he *humbleth* himself before the Father, and *witnesseth* unto the Father that he would be *obedient* unto him in keeping his commandments" (2 Nephi 31:7, italics added). Like Jesus Christ, mortals are baptized in humility and testimony to be obedient to the Father!

Covenant (all forms of the word) is found cover to cover—1 Nephi to Moroni—100 times:
1 Nephi 14:14; 1 Nephi 15:14, 18; 1 Nephi 21:8; 2 Nephi 2:31, 23; 2 Nephi 6:13, 17; 2 Nephi 29:4–5; 2 Nephi 30:2; Enos 1:17; Mosiah 5:5–8; Mosiah 6:1–2; Mosiah 18:10, 13; Mosiah 21:31–32; Mosiah 24:13; Mosiah 26:20; Alma 7:15; Alma 43:11; Alma 44:14–15; Alma 44:19–20; Alma 46:20–22, 31, 35; Alma 53:15–18; Alma 56:6–8; Alma 60:34; Alma 62:16–17; Helaman 1:11; Helaman 2:3; Helaman 6:22; 3 Nephi 5:4–5, 25; 3 Nephi 6:3, 28–30; 3 Nephi 7:11; 3 Nephi 10:7; 3 Nephi 15:8; 3 Nephi 16:5, 11, 12; 3 Nephi 20:12, 22, 25–27, 29, 46; 3 Nephi 21:4, 17; 3 Nephi 21:11; 3 Nephi 21:22; 3 Nephi 22:10; 3 Nephi 24:1; 3 Nephi 29:1, 3, 8–9; Mormon 3:21; Mormon 5:14, 20; Mormon 7:10; Mormon 8:15, 21, 23; Mormon 9:37; Ether 4:15; Ether 13:11; Moroni 10:33.

A Book of Mormon thought about covenant:
The covenant of baptism is the first along the covenant path but not a one and done event. Weekly renewal makes the sacrament a lifetime of recommitting and recovenanting. The resurrected Jesus Christ administered the sacrament

many times during His ministry in ancient America. Of the second time, the record says: "There had been no bread, neither wine, brought by the disciples, neither by the multitude; but he truly gave unto them bread to eat, and also wine to drink" (3 Nephi 20:6–7). In this sacred, miraculous setting, the Lord said: "Behold, ye are the children of the prophets; and ye are of the house of Israel; and ye are of the covenant which the Father made with your fathers, saying unto Abraham: And in thy seed shall all the kindreds of the earth be blessed" (3 Nephi 20:25).

Holy Ghost (all forms of the word) is found cover to cover—1 Nephi to Moroni—94 times:

1 Nephi 10:11, 17, 19, 22; 1 Nephi 11:27; 1 Nephi 12:7, 18; 1 Nephi 13:37; 2 Nephi 26:13; 2 Nephi 28:4, 26, 31; 2 Nephi 31:8, 12–14, 17–18, 21; 2 Nephi 32:2–3, 5; 2 Nephi 33:1; Jacob 6:8; Jacob 5:12–13, 17; Alma 7:10; Alma 8:30; Alma 9:21; Alma 13:12; Alma 34:38; Alma 36:24; Alma 39:5–6; 3 Nephi 9:20; 3 Nephi 11:25, 27, 32, 35–36; 3 Nephi 12:1–2, 6; 3 Nephi 15:23; 3 Nephi 16:4, 6; 3 Nephi 18:37; 3 Nephi 19:9, 13, 20–22; 3 Nephi 20:27; 3 Nephi 21:2; 3 Nephi 26:17; 3 Nephi 27:20; 3 Nephi 28:11, 18; 3 Nephi 29:6; 3 Nephi 30:2; 4 Nephi 1:1, 48; Mormon 1:14; Mormon 7:7, 10; Ether 5:4; Ether 12:14, 23, 41; Moroni 2:2–3; Moroni 3:4; Moroni 6:4, 9; Moroni 7:32, 36, 44; Moroni 8:7, 9, 26, 28; Moroni 10:4–5, 7.

A Book of Mormon thought about Holy Ghost:
Following Jesus's Crucifixion and Resurrection, He ministered to His people in ancient America. During this visit, the disciples "did pray for that which they most desired; and they desired that the Holy Ghost should be given unto them" (3 Nephi 19:7, 9). The text then explains how their prayer was answered. Immediately after the prayer, they went to the edge of a body of water, and Nephi was baptized. Then he baptized the eleven disciples Jesus had chosen. And "when they were all baptized and had come up out of the water, the Holy Ghost did fall upon them, and they were filled with the Holy Ghost and with fire . . . and angels . . . did minister unto them. . . . While the angels were ministering . . . Jesus came and stood in the midst and ministered unto them" (3 Nephi 19:13–15). Praying for the Holy Ghost was prelude to baptism, which was prelude to receiving the Holy Ghost, which was prelude to Jesus appearing. Is there anything we should pray for more than for the constant companionship of the Holy Ghost?

Mercy (all forms of the word) is found cover to cover—1 Nephi to Moroni—84 times:

1 Nephi 1:14; 1 Nephi 8:8; 1 Nephi 21:10, 13; 2 Nephi 2:8, 12; 2 Nephi 4:26; 2 Nephi 9:8; 2 Nephi 9:19, 53; 2 Nephi 11:5; 2 Nephi 19:17; 2 Nephi 24:1; Jacob 4:10; Jacob 6:5; Mosiah 2:39; Mosiah 3:26; Mosiah 4:2; Mosiah 5:15; Mosiah 13:14; Mosiah 15:9; Mosiah 16:1; Mosiah 27:28; Mosiah 28:4; Mosiah 29:20; Alma 2:30; Alma 3:14; Alma 5:4, 6, 33, 48; Alma 7:2, 12; Alma 9:11, 26; Alma 12:33–34; Alma 15:10; Alma 18:41; Alma 19:29; Alma 24:14, 16, 20; Alma 26:37; Alma 32:13, 15–18; Alma 38:7–8, 14; Alma 41:14; Alma 42:1, 15, 21–25, 30–31; Alma 55:23; Helaman 12:6; 3 Nephi 9:14; 3 Nephi 12:7; 3 Nephi 17:7; 3 Nephi 22:8, 10; 3 Nephi 26:5; 3 Nephi 29:7; Mormon 6:22; Ether 11:8; Moroni 7:27; Moroni 8:18; Moroni 9:18, 25.

A Book of Mormon thought about mercy:
The doctrine that mercy is more powerful than justice is taught in Alma 26:17–20. Ammon said:

> *Who could have supposed that our God would have been so merciful as to have snatched us from our awful, sinful, and polluted state? Behold, we went forth even in wrath, with mighty threatenings to destroy his church. Oh then, why did he not consign us to an awful destruction, yea, why did he not let the sword of his justice fall upon us, and doom us to eternal despair? Oh, my soul, almost as it were, fleeth at the thought. Behold, he did not exercise his justice upon us, but in his great mercy hath brought us over that everlasting gulf of death and misery, even to the salvation of our souls.*

Alma told his son Corianton that when a person repents, "mercy [has] claim upon them" (Alma 42:31). I think if *mercy* were capitalized, we would better understand that Jesus Christ is the *Merciful One*; it is through Him that we obtain *mercy.*

Resurrection (all forms of the word) is found cover to cover—1 Nephi to Moroni—81 times:

2 Nephi 2:8; 2 Nephi 9:6, 12, 22; 2 Nephi 10:25; 2 Nephi 26:3; Jacob 4:11–12; Jacob 6:9; Mosiah 13:35; Mosiah 15:20–22, 24, 26; Mosiah 16:7–8, 11; Mosiah 18:2, 9; Mosiah 26:2; Alma 4:14; Alma 11:45; Alma 12:8, 24–25; Alma 16:19–20; Alma 21:9; Alma 27:28; Alma 33:22; Alma 40:1–3, 6–7, 9, 11, 14–21; Alma 41:2; Alma 42:23; Helaman 14:15–17; 3 Nephi 6:20; 3 Nephi 26:5; Mormon 7:6; Moroni 7:41; Moroni 9:13.

A Book of Mormon thought about resurrection:
Without the Resurrection we would, according to Moroni, be in an endless sleep. Because of the Resurrection of Jesus Christ, "all men shall be awakened by the power of God when the trump shall sound; and they shall come forth, both small and great, and all shall stand before his bar, being redeemed and loosed from this eternal band of death, which death is a temporal death" (Mormon 9:13). Because of the Resurrection of Jesus Christ, "The soul shall be restored to the body, and the body to the soul; yea, and every limb and joint shall be restored to its body; yea, even a hair of the head shall not be lost; but all things shall be restored to their proper and perfect frame" (Alma 40:23). It is likely that at every Latter-day Saint funeral you attend, verses from Alma, Moroni, and Mormon will be quoted.

Prophet (all forms of the word) is found cover to cover—1 Nephi to Moroni—187 times:

1 Nephi 1:4, 20; 1 Nephi 2:13; 1 Nephi 3:18, 20; 1 Nephi 5:13; 1 Nephi 7:14; 1 Nephi 10:5; 1 Nephi 10:4–5, 7; 1 Nephi 11:27; 1 Nephi 13:23, 39; 1 Nephi 19:4, 11–17, 20–21, 23–24; 1 Nephi 22:2, 15, 17, 20–21, 23; 2 Nephi 2:30; 2 Nephi 6:12, 14; 2 Nephi 9:2; 2 Nephi 13:2; 2 Nephi 19:17, 19, 28; 2 Nephi 25:5, 9, 18–19, 28; 2 Nephi 26:3, 5, 8; 2 Nephi 27:5; 2 Nephi 31:4; Jacob 4:4, 6, 13–14; Jacob 5:1–2; Jacob 6:1, 8; Jacob 7:11; Enos 1:22; Jarom 1:10–11; Words of Mormon 1:3, 16, 18; Mosiah 2:34; Mosiah 3:13, 15, 22; Mosiah 7:6; Mosiah 8:15–16; Mosiah 13:33; Mosiah 15:11, 13, 22; Mosiah 18:19; Alma 5:11, 24; Alma 7:25; Alma 8:20, Alma 10:7; Alma 18:36; Alma 19:4; Alma 20:15; Alma 30:6, 14, 22, 44; Alma 33:3, 17; Alma 37:30; Alma 40:22, 24; Helaman preface; Helaman 8:9, 16, 19–20; Helaman 9:2, 16, 27, 40; Helaman 11:18, 22; Helaman 13:24–27, 33; Helaman 15:7, 11; Helaman 16:13; 3 Nephi 1:4, 9, 13, 16, 18, 20, 26; 3 Nephi 2:7; 3 Nephi 3:19; 3 Nephi 5:1–2; 3 Nephi 6:25; 3 Nephi 7:6, 10, 14; 3 Nephi 8:3, 25; 3 Nephi 9:5, 7–11; 3 Nephi 10:11–12, 14, 16; 3 Nephi 11:10, 15; 3 Nephi 12:12, 17; 3 Nephi 14:12, 15; 3 Nephi 15:6, 10; 3 Nephi 16:17; 3 Nephi 20:23–25; 3 Nephi 23:5; 3 Nephi 29:2; 4 Nephi 1:34; Mormon 2:10; Ether 7:23–25; Ether 8:25; Ether 9:28–29; Ether 11:1–2, 5, 12–13, 20, 22; Ether 12:2, 41; Ether 15:3; Moroni 7:23; Moroni 8:29.

A Book of Mormon thought about prophet:
Abinadi outlined some responsibilities of prophets—past, present, and future. They "have published peace . . . brought good tidings of good . . .

published salvation; and said unto Zion: Thy God reigneth! And O how beautiful upon the mountains were their feet! And again, how beautiful upon the mountains are the feet of those that are still publishing peace! And again, how beautiful upon the mountains are the feet of those who shall hereafter publish peace, yea, from this time henceforth and forever" (Mosiah 15:14–17). This is one of the clearest teachings that the prophets have been called of God in every dispensation—past, present, and future. Prophets were, prophets are, and prophets will be spokesmen proclaiming the gospel of Jesus Christ.

A thought about hope, *which is found 60 times, 1 Nephi to Moroni:*
It is one thing to write about hope when things are going well, but when their entire civilization is being destroyed before their eyes, Mormon and Moroni still cling to hope, making their words that much more notable. Mormon wrote a letter that Moroni included in his own book: "Wherefore, my beloved brethren, pray unto the Father with all the energy of heart . . . that we may have this hope" (Moroni 7:48). At his darkest moments, Mormon uses the word *hope* twelve times that chapter. Moroni, the lone survivor, uses *hope* eight times in Ether 12. In the final chapter of the Book of Mormon, Moroni describes the result of living without hope: "And if ye have no hope ye must needs be in despair; and despair cometh because of iniquity" (Moroni 10:22).

A thought about faith, *which is found 262 times 1 Nephi to Moroni:*
Ether 12, written by Moroni in the Book of Mormon, is similar to Hebrews 11, written by the Apostle Paul in the New Testament. Both men list foundations of their faith as evidences for their faith. Moroni uses *faith* thirty-eight times in his chapter and Paul uses *faith* twenty-six times in his chapter. Both men cite miraculous events of the past as personal touchstones.

Another look at faith and how it works is in the book of Jarom. It is only one chapter, but in Jarom's few words, he uses *faith* three times. "And there are many among us who have many revelations, for they are not all stiffnecked. And as many as are not stiffnecked and have faith, have communion with the Holy Spirit, which maketh manifest unto the children of men, according to their faith" (Jarom 1:4). This is an if/then promise: If you have faith and are not stiffnecked or prideful, then you have communion with the Holy Spirit.

Jarom further teaches how societies prosper by faith: "Our kings and our leaders were mighty men in the faith of the Lord; and they taught the people the ways of the Lord; wherefore, we withstood the Lamanites and swept them away out of our lands, and began to fortify our cities, or whatsoever place of our inheritance. And we multiplied exceedingly, and spread upon the face of the land, and became exceedingly rich in gold, and in silver, and in precious things, and in fine workmanship of wood, in buildings, and in machinery, and also in iron and copper, and brass and steel, making all manner of tools of every kind to till the ground, and weapons of war—yea, the sharp pointed arrow, and the quiver, and the dart, and the javelin, and all preparations for war" (Jarom 1:7–8).

A thought about repentance, *which is found 361 times 1 Nephi to Moroni:*
I would never rejoice in another's sin, but in the case of Alma's son Corianton, how blessed we are to have Alma's counsel to his son. Had Corianton not sinned, his father's blessing would have been similar to Helaman's and Shiblon's—shorter and more upbeat. Alma acknowledged this to Corianton who may have observed his brothers' blessings: "And now, my son, I have somewhat more to say unto thee than what I said unto thy brother[s]" (Alma 39:1). In his blessing to Corianton, Alma uses some form of the word *repent* twenty times. He closes the blessing with these words: "And now, my son, I desire that ye should let these things trouble you no more, and only let your sins trouble you, with that trouble which shall bring you down unto repentance. O my son, I desire that ye should deny the justice of God no more. Do not endeavor to excuse yourself in the least point because of your sins, by denying the justice of God; but do you let the justice of God, and his mercy, and his long-suffering have full sway in your heart; and let it bring you down to the dust in humility. And now, O my son, ye are called of God to preach the word unto this people. And now, my son, go thy way, declare the word with truth and soberness, that thou mayest bring souls unto repentance, that the great plan of mercy may have claim upon them. And may God grant unto you even according to my words. Amen" (Alma 42: 29–31). Corianton did repent and was a faithful missionary.

Summary
I bear witness of the magnitude and power of the doctrine of Jesus Christ, doctrine that is testified of and augmented every time the word is used—*baptism* 145 times, *covenant* 154 times, *Holy Ghost* 94 times, *mercy* 84 times, *resurrection* 81 times, *prophet* 187 times, *hope* 60 times, *faith* 262 times, and *repentance* 361 times, and many, many more. I pray the clear and consistent

doctrine that adds truth upon truth and evidence upon evidence will awe, inspire, and testify to you.

All this and more in 65 working days.

Unique Vocabularies

MY LINGUISTIC EXAMINATION OF THE Book of Mormon began when a series of experiences led me to type the Book of Mormon as a new way to study it. I began on January 13, 2010, and typed the title page, the Introduction, the Testimony of Three Witnesses, and the Testimony of Eight Witnesses. August 1, 2011, a year and a half and 531 pages later, I typed Moroni's last words. I had typed all 268,163 words in the Book of Mormon, plus all the introductory pages and headnotes—everything but the footnotes. But I almost didn't make it. After about eight months, I almost quit.

I had typed from 1 Nephi through Mosiah 29, which took me to page 207. The longest book in the Book of Mormon, the book of Alma, loomed before me. Although I had learned and felt much, Alma with its 63 chapters and 162 pages seemed daunting. Over and over I had to refuse to listen to the negative voice whispering in my ear to abandon the project. After a week in limbo, I felt something propel me to forge ahead. As I began to type Alma 1, I almost immediately noticed that individual words seemed to call attention to themselves. Thoughts came, such as *I don't remember typing that word before* and *This text feels different somehow*. After typing more than two hundred pages, I could tell something had changed. I couldn't identify what it was, so I started typing Alma 1 again. I was on the alert for anything that might have triggered my feelings.

I typed Alma 1:1. "Now it came to pass that in the first year of the reign of the judges over the people of Nephi, from this time forward, king Mosiah having gone the way of all the earth, having warred . . ." I paused. I couldn't think of a scripture that contained the word *warred* and couldn't recall typing it. I typed w-a-r-r-e-d into a scripture search program and saw it is found ten times—nine times in the Old Testament and once in the Book of Mormon, of course in Alma 1:1. Then just two words after *warred*, I saw the word *warfare* and typed it into the scripture program. It is found eight times: two times in the Old Testament, three in the New Testament, and three in the Book of Mormon—all three in the book of Alma. As I continued, I kept typing more and more words looking for those that are found for the first or only time in Alma 1. Below are the first six verses of Alma with the unique words in bold italics. With every unique word I found, my surprise and anticipation grew.

THE BOOK OF ALMA
THE SON OF ALMA

1. Now it came to pass that in the first year of the reign of the judges over the people of Nephi, from this time forward, king Mosiah having gone the way of all the earth, having **warred** a good **warfare**, walking uprightly before God, **leaving** none to reign in his stead; nevertheless he had established laws, and they were **acknowledged** by the people; therefore they were obliged to abide by the laws which he had made.

2. And it came to pass that in the first year of the reign of Alma in the judgment-seat, there was a man brought before him to be judged, a man who was large, and was **noted** for his much strength.

3. And he had gone about among the people, preaching to them that which he **termed** to be the word of God, **bearing down** against the church; declaring unto the people that every priest and teacher ought to become popular; and they ought not to labor with their hands, but that they ought to be supported by the people.

4. And he also testified unto the people that all mankind should be saved at the last day, and that they need not fear nor tremble, but that they might lift up their heads and rejoice; for the Lord had created all men, and had also redeemed all men; and, in the end, all men should have eternal life.

5. And it came to pass that he did teach these things so much that many did believe on his words, even so many that they began to support him and give him money.

6. And he began to be lifted up in the pride of his heart, and to wear very **costly** apparel, yea, and even began to establish a church after the manner of his preaching.

By the end of Alma 1, I had forty-six unique words on the list. I returned to Mosiah 29 to see if it contained any unique words. There were thirty. What I had considered a project now felt like a mission to find more and more unique words. The journey had begun.

Ten months later, when I had finished typing the entire Book of Mormon, I realized that at no point in the Book of Mormon are the differences in two prophets' vocabularies better shown than in Mosiah 29 and Alma 1. This awareness humbled me. I describe the entire experience as "gloriously labor intensive." I testify that in-depth scripture study invites the guidance and influence of Holy Ghost.

Oliver Cowdery describes his glorious experience as Joseph's scribe: "These were days never to be forgotten—to sit under the sound of a voice dictated by the inspiration of heaven, awakened the utmost gratitude of this bosom! Day after day I continued, uninterrupted, to write from his mouth, as he translated with the Urim and Thummim, or, as the Nephites would have said, 'Interpreters,' the history or record called 'The Book of Mormon'" (Joseph Smith—History, following verse 75).

This was a gloriously labor-intensive experience. It took me 565 days, five hundred days longer than for Joseph and his scribes to complete the Book of Mormon. Besides typing, the hundreds of extra days were spent looking up all the words I suspected might be unique. There are over five thousand unique words in the Book of Mormon, including proper nouns. It was a huge undertaking.

The miracle of finding unique words in an edited and abridged book is possible simply because the prophets/editors/abridgers of the Book of Mormon did their job. An editor's purpose is to preserve the author's style and vocabulary as much as possible. For example, for 55 percent of Mosiah, Mormon copied first person point of view excerpts from the teachings of King Benjamin, King Zeniff, the prophets Abinadi, Alma, Alma the younger, and King Mosiah." An abridger abbreviates, again trying to preserve as much of the original as possible. As Mormon abridged Mosiah, he "used just over 31,000 words to recount 49 years of Nephite history. . . . For about 45% of Mosiah, Mormon wrote third person point of view summaries . . . as well as adding his own editorial comments" (https://ca.churchofjesuschrist.org/mormon-the-chief-editor-of-the-book-of-mormon-part-2).

I realized that whatever my experience typing the Book of Mormon was, it was nothing like Oliver's, and whatever Oliver's was, it was nothing like Joseph's. Only Joseph knew the intricacies of how Reformed Egyptian on the gold plates became English in the Book of Mormon. In 1840, he said the words were "communicated to him, direct from heaven . . . as dictated by God" (Andrew F. Ehat and Lyndon W. Cook, comps., *The Words of Joseph Smith*, Religious Studies Monograph Series 6 [Salt Lake City: Bookcraft, 1980], xx). On this topic, the sixth president of the Church, Joseph F. Smith (1838–1918), said: "Some persons have thought that the Lord revealed to Joseph the ideas, and that Joseph conveyed those ideas into the English language. But this is not so. The Lord gave not only the ideas but the language itself—the very words" (Joseph F. Smith, "The Territorial Inquirer," March 2, 1881). A modern scholar on the Book of Mormon, Dr. Royal Skousen, wrote: There is "strong support for the hypothesis that Joseph Smith was given the text word for word" (Royal Skousen, *The Book of Mormon, The Earliest Text*, second edition, xvii).

Finally, I finished. It was at this point that I started connecting the unique words to the individuals who used them. I saw that Nephi used 140 unique words, Alma 271, and Isaiah 297. However, these big numbers are no more impressive than some small numbers. For example, the father of King Lamoni, whose name is not given in the Book of Mormon, used three unique words—*generosity, insist,* and *rooted.* Even more noteworthy is that *generosity* and *insist* are only found in these singular instances.

At one point in King Benjamin's sermon, he asks the people how they feel about what he just taught. They answer aloud with one voice, using a unique word: "O have mercy, and apply the atoning blood of Christ that we may receive forgiveness of our sins" (Mosiah 4:2). The word *apply* is found only once in the Book of Mormon.

The fact that there are unique vocabularies amazes me and is convincing evidence that the Book of Mormon was not written by Joseph Smith. Joseph didn't think up 140 unique words for Nephi or think to have a large congregation say in unison *apply* and use it only once.

For modern readers of the Book of Mormon, this evidence is probably easier to grasp because of our familiarity with translation technology. Regardless, it was not a technological feat but a revelatory process. We know this because there is historical evidence in manuscripts, physical evidence in the Book of Mormon itself, and spiritual evidence in the confirmation of the Holy Ghost. The Book of Mormon is a divinely generous gift from God to His spiritually thirsty children. It is a call to repentance to a wicked generation. How blessed we are.

Book of Mormon people—Number of unique words:

Abinadi 19	Ammon1 1
Alma1 19	Ammon2 34
Alma2 271	Amulek 20
Amaleki 3	Angel of the Lord 7

Brother of Jared 2
Enos 7
Ether 62
Gideon 4
Gideon's men 1
Giddonah 1
Giddianhi 3
Gidgiddoni 2
God/Lord 2
Helaman2 167
Helaman3 35
Isaiah 297
Jacob 76
Jarom 9
Jesus Christ 5
John the Baptist 2
King Benjamin 41
King Benjamin people 1
King Lamoni 13
King Lamoni's servants 1
King Lamoni's wife 3
King Lamoni's father 3
King Limhi 23
King Noah 2
King Noah people 1

Korihor 2
Laman and Lemuel 4
Lamanite Guards and
  Aminadab 2
Lehi 28
Malachi 17
Mormon 75
Captain Moroni 38
Moroni 51
Mosiah 24
Nephi1 140
Nephi2 47
Nephi3 79
Nephi4 10
Nephite Soldiers 3
Omni 1
Pahoran 8
Samuel the Lamanite 16
Sariah 2
Sherem 1
Shiblon 2
Unbelievers 3
Zeezrom 1
Zeniff 15
Zenos 19

All this and more in 65 working days.

Evidence 6
Joseph Smith's Unique Vocabulary

AFTER TYPING, IDENTIFYING, AND COUNTING unique words in the Book of Mormon, I found 57 individual vocabularies, showing the Book of Mormon is not in Joseph Smith's vocabulary. I did the same with the Pearl of Great Price because I had a question. Since the books of Moses and Abraham and the inspired revision of Matthew 23–24 were revealed to Joseph Smith, I wanted to know if it was all in Joseph's vocabulary. Would there be any unique words as there were in the Book of Mormon? That is, when God, Moses, and Satan speak in the first chapter of Moses, are they words Joseph thought they might have said or are they the actual words of God, Moses, and Satan?

In typing the Pearl of Great Price, I discovered 24 individual vocabularies: Moses, God the Father, Jesus Christ, Adam, Eve, Enoch, Cain, Abel, Satan, an angel, the Earth, Lamech, Mahijah, Noah, Abraham, Matthew, John the Baptist, Malachi, Martin Harris, Oliver Cowdery, three groups of people in Enoch's time, and Joseph Smith in Joseph Smith—History. (At the end of this chapter, I've included a list of these individuals and the number of unique words each used.) A comparison between the Pearl of Great Price and Joseph Smith—History may seem limited because they are both so short. The Pearl of Great Price is sixty-one pages and Joseph Smith—History is thirteen of those pages. However, the results show that the length doesn't matter.

The moment of truth came when I had finished typing the Pearl of Great Price except for Joseph Smith—History and the Articles of Faith. I would soon know if the books of Moses, Abraham, and Matthew were in their own words or paraphrased by Joseph. It would have been okay if it were all in Joseph's vocabulary, but I hoped for more evidences, more unique words. I started to breathe again when I found Joseph's first three unique words. I was happy. Soon happiness turned to amazement and amazement to awe as the list kept growing. Final count: Joseph Smith—History has 477 unique words compared to the rest of the Pearl of Great Price. Of the 477 words, 152 are unique in all scripture, which means, 152 of Joseph's words in Joseph Smith—History are not found in the Old or New Testaments, Book of Mormon, or the rest of the Pearl of Great Price. These I call super unique words. In the list below, they are in solid capital letters.

There is one caveat. Although I assumed that Joseph Smith—History was all in his own words, I realize scribes and editors can influence dictated documents and original drafts. Sidney Rigdon and George Robinson helped Joseph with his history. Later James Mulholland copied the words into Joseph's manuscript history, and Willard Richards edited the account. How much these men influenced the published account is unknown. However, because 477 words is so many, a few words here or there make no difference.

(Please forgive any errors. I have checked and rechecked many times.) I hope this evidence is clear. The ancient documents Joseph Smith brought to the world are not written in his vocabulary. He received them through revelation by the mercy, gift, and power of God.

Joseph Smith's unique vocabulary in Joseph Smith—History compared to the rest of the Pearl of Great Price:
Abandon, ABOVE-MENTIONED, acquainted, ACTIVE, ACTUAL, ACTUALLY, ADDRESSED, adversary, affected, AFFECTIONATE, AFFIRM, afflictions, AFOREMENTIONED, ALERT, allowed, aloof, ancient, ankles, ANNOYER, ANXIETIES, appeal, appearing, approaching, around, ARRANGEMENTS, AMIDST, arrival, arrived, ascended, ASSERT, ASSOCIATED, astonishment, attain, attended, attention, ATTRACT, AUTHORS, bed, BEDSIDE, BEHAVIOR, BETOOK, BIBLES, board, bottom, bound, bows, breastplate, brightness, BRILLIANT, building, carelessly, CAUTION, cement, certain, chapter, character, charge, charges, CHEERY, CIRCULATING, CIRCULATION, circumstances, classes, CLERGY, clothing, cock, combine, comfortable, commenced, commit, common, communication, company, CONCLUDING, conclusion, condemnation, condemned, conducted, conduit, confession, confidence, confusion, consequence, considerable, CONSTITUTED, contempt, contending, CONTESTS, continuing, CONTINUOUS, convenient, conversing, conversion, convert, converted, converts, COUNTERACTED, county, CROSSWAYS, CROWED, daily, DARED, day's, deal, decided, defense, defy, DELUDED, DENOMINATIONS, deposited,

DESIGNED, desires, desolations, despair, DESTINED, determination, different, DIFFERENTLY, digging, directed, directs, DISABUSE, DISAPPEARED, discover, dishonest, displayed, DISPOSED, disposition, DISPROVE, distinctly, DISTINCTNESS, DISTRICT, DISTURBER, Divine, divine, division, doctrines, dollars, doomed, during, duty, earthly, edge, edges, ELEVATED, elsewhere, employed, enabled, endeavoring, ENDEAVORS, enemy, enlightened, enough, ENSUING, entirely, equally, errors, establish, EVERYBODY, EVIL-DISPOSED, exactly, EXCITE, EXCITED, EXCITEMENT, EXERTING, EXERTION, EXERTIONS, EXHAUSTED, experienced, EXPLANATIONS, expressed, exquisite, EXTRAORDINARY, extreme, failed, FAITHS, FALSEHOODS, FARMED, feeling, feelings, feet, fence, file, finally, FIREPLACE, floor, FOIBLES, forbade, force, forced, former, FREQUENTLY, friend, friendly, friends, GENTLEMAN, glorify, glorious, GRADUALLY, guilty, happened, heavenly, heavy, helpless, HIGH STANDING, HIRING, human, IMAGINARY, imperfections, importance, impossible, IMPRESSIONS, INCESSANT, increase, INDUCED, infancy, influence, INFLUENCED, informed, INQUIRERS, INQUIRIES, instantly, instruction, intelligence, intention, intentions, INTERRUPTION, INTERVENED, INTERVIEWS, INTOLERABLE, invented, IRRELIGIOUS, join, joined, JOVIAL, kindly, kindreds, kinds, kneeled, laboring, labors, lack, lacked, latest, latter-day, lay, leaned, least, legs, length, LEVER, LEVITY, liberally, lighted, lighter, lightly, lightning, limited, lips, loose, mad, maintained, maintenance, MALIGNANT, manifestation, manifested, married, marveling, marvelous, meaning, MEANTIME, meditation, meetings, mentioned, messenger, middle, MILITATE, MINGLING, MOBBED, MOBBING, MOBS, MONEY-DIGGER, MOTIVE, multitudes, musing, mysterious, native, nearly, necessary, necessity, neck, neglect, neighborhood, noonday, object, obscure, obtained, obtaining, occupied, offend, OFFENSIVE, opinions, opportunity, opposed, opposition, organization, otherwise, overwhelmed, OWING, part, parties, PARTY, passages, period, permit, persecute, persecuted, persecution, person, Personage, personage, PERSONAGES, persons, pestilence, pillar, plates, POIGNANT, pointing, ponder, popular, precisely, PREJUDICE, preparing, PREVALENT, previous, previously, PROBABILITY, proceedings, PROFESSORS, progress, promised, PROMOTING, proper, prophecies, PROSELYTED, protected, protection, providence, public, quite, QUOTED, QUOTING, reading, READS, reality, reclaimed, RECOLLECT, RECOLLECTS, recovering,

REFLECTED, REFLECTION, region, rehearse, rehearsed, relate, related, relation, RELATIVE, RELIGIONISTS, religious, REMOVAL, render, REPEAT, REPLIED, REPORTS, required, resided, RESIDENT, resorted, RESPECTABILITY, respecting, RESPECTIVE, RESPONSIBLE, retired, returned, reviled, reviling, RIDICULED, robe, ROUNDING, RUIN, RUMOR, safe, satisfied, SCANTY, scarcely, scene, school, scripture, scriptures, SECTARIAN, SECTS, SEEMINGLY, seized, serious, service, SETTLING, several, severe, shortly, silver, SINGULARITY, sink, society, somewhat, sooner, source, start, started, state, stir, STRANGENESS, stratagem, STRENUOUS, strict, success, suffering, sufficient, supplication, suppose, surprised, teaching, telling, TEMPERAMENT, tempt, temptations, tenets, thick, THINNER, THOUSANDTH, threatened, TOWNSHIP, translating, transpired, treated, tumult, UNABLE, UNACQUAINTED, UNCONSCIOUS, UNDERTAKING, UNEASINESS, united, unlawful, UNSEEN, UNUSUAL, upbraid, upbraided, upbraideth, USUAL, VARIATION, venture, verse, village, visited, VOCALLY, VOCATIONS, VOLUMES, wasted, weakness, whiteness, withstand, woods, worldly, WRIST, wrong, zeal, zealous.

At this point, I had another question. I was curious to know how many of these words were also in the Book of Mormon. Even though there are 57 unique vocabularies, could Joseph's own vocabulary also be found in the Book of Mormon? So I looked up every word again. I didn't know what I would find because many of them are everyday words. But of the 477, 238 are not found in the Book of Mormon but are in the Old and/or New Testaments and/or Doctrine and Covenants! More convincing evidence.

Joseph Smith's unique vocabulary not in the Book of Mormon

Above-mentioned, active, actual, actually, addressed, affected, affectionate, affirm, aforementioned, alert, allowed, aloof, amidst, annoyer, anxieties, arrangements, arrival, assert, associated, attract, authors, bedside, behavior, betook, bibles, board, brilliant, carelessly, caution, chapter, character, cheery, circulating, circulation, clergy, cock, comfortable, concluding, conclusion, confession, consequence, constituted, contests, continuous, convenient, converts, counteracted, county, crossways, crowed, dared, decided, defense, deluded, denominations, designed, desolations, destined, differently, directs, disabuse, disappeared, disapprove, dishonest, displayed, disposed, distinctly, distinctness, district, disturber, divine, Divine, dollars, doomed, earthly, edges, elevated, elsewhere, enabled, endeavors, ensuing, equally, everybody, evil-disposed, exactly, excite, excited, excitement, exertion, exertions, exhausted, experienced, explanations, extraordinary, failed, faiths, falsehoods, farmed, fence, file, fireplace, foibles, forced, frequently, gentleman, gradually, high-standing, hiring, imaginary, impressions, incessant, induced, influence, influenced, inquirers, inquiries, instantly, intelligence, interruption, intervened, interviews, intolerable, invented, irreligious, jovial, kindly, lack, lacked, latest, Latter-day, leaned, lever, levity, lighter, limited, malignant, meantime, meditation, mentioned, militate, mingling, mobbed, mobbing, mobs, money-digger, motive, musing, native, necessity, neighborhood, noonday, obscure, occupied, offensive, opinions, organization, overwhelmed, owing, party, passages, permit, personage, Personage, Personages, poignant, precisely, prejudice, prevalent, previously, probability, professors, promoting, proselyted, public, quite, quoted, quoting, reads, recollect, recollects, recovering, reflected, reflection, relation, relative, religionists, religious, removal, repeat, replied, reports, resided, resident, respectability, respecting, respective, responsible, ridiculed, rounding, ruin, rumor, scanty, scarcely, school, sectarian, sects, seemingly, settling, singularity, strangeness, strenuous, surprised, temperament, tenets, thickened, thinner, township, tumult, unable, unacquainted, unconscious, undertaking, uneasiness, unlawful, unseen, unusual, upbraid, upbraided, upbraideth, usual, variation, verse, vocally, vocations, volumes, woods, worldly, wrist.

I find it impossible to explain where the Book of Mormon, the book of Moses, the book of Abraham, and the changes to Matthew 23–24 came from except by "the mercy of God, by the power of God" (D&C 1:29) through Joseph—prophet, seer, and revelator. The unique vocabularies in the Book of Mormon testify that the Book of Mormon was not written by Joseph Smith. The unique vocabularies in the Pearl of Great Price verify that it is not written by Joseph Smith. Moses's words are Moses's, Abraham's words are Abraham's. The only words in Joseph's own vocabulary are those he wrote himself about his life in Joseph Smith—History as printed in The Pearl of Great Price. These unique words testify to the power of the Lord's prophetic mantle on a young man who the historians say had a third-grade education.

Unique Vocabularies in The Pearl of Great Price
Moses 127, God (in Moses) 33, Jesus Christ (in Moses) 57, Adam 2, Eve 3, Enoch 31, Cain 9, Abel 3, Angel 1, Earth 4, Lamech 2, Mahijah 2, Noah

2, Group A 1, Group B 4, Group C 3, Abraham 75, Satan 1, Matthew and Jesus (in Matthew 23–24) 60, John the Baptist 4, Malachi 9, Martin Harris 20, Oliver Cowdery 115, Joseph Smith 477.

All this and more in 65 working days.

Evidence 7
Punctuation

WHO WOULD THINK THAT THE lack of punctuation in the original manuscript of the Book of Mormon is evidence of the truthfulness of the Book of Mormon? Joseph did not dictate to Oliver: "I *comma* Nephi *comma* having been born of goodly parents *comma* therefore I was taught somewhat in all the learning of my father *semicolon* . . ." Below is an unpunctuated passage from 1 Nephi 8:16–21 to give you a feeling for what the text looked like from Joseph's dictation to Oliver's pen to the Grandin Print Shop, where it was punctuated and typeset:

> *and it came to pass that they did come unto me and partake of the fruit also and it came to pass that I was desirous that Laman and Lemuel should come and partake of the fruit also wherefore I cast mine eyes towards the head of the river that perhaps I might see them and it came to pass that I saw them but they would not come unto me and partake of the fruit and I beheld a rod of iron and it extended along the bank of the river and led to the tree by which I stood and I also beheld a strait and narrow path which came along by the rod of iron even to the tree by which I stood and it also led by the head of the fountain unto a large and spacious field as if it had been a world and I saw numberless concourses of people many of whom were pressing forward that they might obtain the path which led unto the tree by which I stood*

The fact that there is no punctuation is another evidence that the coming forth of the Book of Mormon happened just as Joseph Smith said. The oldest known document using punctuation is from the ninth century, relatively modern compared to the Book of Mormon. Moroni put the golden plates in the stone box about AD 421. It's interesting to note that the Dead Sea Scrolls, written between 150 BC and AD 70, also have no punctuation.

Ninth-century punctuation used dots between words and horizontal strokes between thoughts. A variety of such methods were used to help readers make sense of written text and understand the author's intent. It was not until about the year 1440 that punctuation began to be standardized. This coincided with the invention of the Gutenberg Press.

There is a type of punctuation in the unpunctuated Book of Mormon, however, that helps readers pause and make sense of the text. I refer to them as internal markers. A few of them include "now therefore," "and thus we see," "and again," "for behold," and "it came to pass." It is interesting that in the unpunctuated sample text above, "it came to pass," is found three times.

You may be wondering when and by whom the Book of Mormon was punctuated. John Gilbert, an employee of E. B. Grandin, added punctuation as he typeset. Mr. Gilbert said: "Every chapter, if I remember correctly, was one solid paragraph, without a punctuation mark, from beginning to end. . . . I punctuated it to read as I supposed the author intended" https://scholarsarchive.byu.edu/cgi/viewcontent.cgi?article=1506&context=jbms). Some of his punctuation has been changed in subsequent editions, but a statement on the Church website acknowledges Mr. Gilbert's work: "Although Gilbert did a fine job adding 30,000 to 35,000 punctuation marks to the text, some errors were inevitable" https://history.churchofjesuschrist.org/content/museum/the-book-of-mormon-from-manuscript-to-press?lang=eng).

Oliver Cowdery also did a fine job creating the printer's manuscript by copying from the original, but errors were made. What is obvious from the fact that Oliver made a second copy is that the Book of Mormon was worth that much effort. Picture the scene: Joseph and Oliver have just finished translating the Book of Mormon. Oliver's handwritten pages number about 480. Joseph has returned the plates to Moroni. Oliver is rejoicing that the manuscript is finished, but Joseph's anxiety for its safety is increasing. He has learned by sad experience of the need for a backup copy because of the loss of the 116 pages. Think of the possible conversation between Joseph and Oliver: "Oliver, thank you for your faithful service. The manuscript is complete. How grateful I am for your help, but I feel the need for a second copy. Will you please write it again?" However Joseph may have phrased the question, Oliver said yes, which means he wrote the Book of Mormon, as it is today, about 1.85 times. Oliver's willingness to create a second copy is *his* singular testimony of the truthfulness of the Book of Mormon.

How likely is it that Joseph knew ancient documents had no punctuation? Zero! The lack of punctuation is one more thing Joseph couldn't have known but got right in 65 working days.

Evidence 8
Four Thousand Changes

THERE HAVE BEEN SEVEN MAJOR editions of the Book of Mormon published by the Church. "The purpose of each new edition is to eliminate the human errors that have occurred. This is all aimed at bringing the text into conformity with the message and meaning of the original manuscripts. The various editorial changes that have been made, such as typographical, grammatical and syntactical changes, have improved readability while leaving the doctrine unaltered" (https://newsroom.churchofjesuschrist. org/article/understanding-the-process-of-publishing-the-book-of-mormon). Since the first edition, there have been more than four thousand changes.

Anti-Mormons use these four thousand changes as something that should challenge a person's belief in the Book of Mormon. They say so many changes indicate that the book cannot be true. Actually, the four thousand changes are unrelated to its truthfulness. Spelling and grammatical errors don't make something untrue. Being tired, hungry, or rushed—all human aspects of daily life—increased the probability of error. Joseph recognized the human-error factor in the first edition and authorized over a thousand changes. Before the second edition in 1837, Joseph and Oliver proofread the original manuscript of the Book of Mormon to correct errors. "Joseph Smith authorized and made close to 1,000 changes. . . . While some critics cite these textual errors to challenge the Book of Mormon's authenticity, scholars with experience in translation see them as natural consequences of human imperfections" (ibid). You will recall that the Book of Mormon was printed mainly from the printer's manuscript, the backup copy Oliver Cowdery made at Joseph's request. Fewer errors would have occurred if the original manuscript had been used.

Errors are inevitable in every book. I remember reading that a book should have no more than three errors per ten thousand words to be considered professional. One online fiction editor says the industry standard is to provide manuscripts that are 95% error-free (https://www.lisagilliam.

com/proofreading). Errors in fiction don't matter that much, but we expect scripture to be error free. Though scripture comes from God, the moment a human touches it, errors are inevitable. "Though it is the most important book in the religious life and culture of the English-speaking world, the King James Bible or Authorized Version of 1611 has never been perfectly printed," wrote David Norton, a professor at Victoria University" (https://newsroom.churchofjesuschrist.org/article/understanding-the-process-of-publishing-the-book-of-mormon).

The more than 4,000 changes to the Book of Mormon fall into three categories:

1.   Errors made when a scribe heard a word incorrectly.

In Dr. Royal Skousen's book, he gives this example. Christian Whitmer was scribing in 1 Nephi 7:5. The original manuscript reads, "The Lord did soften the heart of Ishmael and also his hole hole." When Oliver Cowdery copied the text into the printer's manuscript, he interpreted "hole hole" as a mistake for "household." After studying similar passages, Dr. Skousen thinks the first *hole* should have been *whole* and the second should have been *household*. The passage would then read, "The Lord did soften the heart of Ishmael and also his whole household" (*The Book of Mormon, The Earliest Text, Second Edition* [Yale University Press, 2022], xii).

2.   Errors Dr. Skousen believes Oliver made that remain in the 1981 edition. His research shows these three sentences should read differently. I include these here for interest only, not to support his point that they should be changed.

- 1 Nephi 8:31: "And he also saw other multitudes *pressing* their way towards that great and spacious building" rather than "feeling their way."
- 2 Nephi 1:5: "The Lord hath *consecrated*" should replace *covenanted*. Here is the text of the verse, so you can see that the meaning is clearer when the change is made. "Covenanted" is used two times in the verse. It is the second time that should be changed. "But, said he, notwithstanding our afflictions, we have obtained a land of promise, a land which is choice above all other lands; a land which the Lord God hath covenanted with me should be a land for the inheritance of my seed. Yea, the Lord hath covenanted [*consecrated*] this land unto me, and to my children forever, and also all those who should be led out of other countries by the hand of the Lord."

3. Errors John Gilbert made while typesetting the first edition.

    *   "One of the bigger errors occurred on the title page, which includes the preface. . . . Without any punctuation and not understanding the history or content of the Book of Mormon, Gilbert broke the paragraphs in the wrong place, disconnecting 'the book of Ether' from 'the people of Jared.' This was corrected in the 1837 edition" (https://history.churchofjesuschrist.org/content/museum/the-book-of-mormon-from-manuscript-to-press?lang=eng#).
    *   "Oliver's handwriting also presented a special challenge to the typesetter. His *R* (which looks like a 'Palmer' *R*) and his *N* are difficult to distinguish, as are his *B* and *L*. So in the first edition, Gadianton was mislabeled 'the *nobler*,' rather than 'the *robber*.' In a similar way, the typesetter apparently mistook Oliver's *RM* as *UN*. So in 1 Nephi 13, where the original manuscript read *formation,* the typesetter misread *founation.* Then, thinking the letter *d* had been left out, he supplied it. In the 1981 edition, *foundation* has been corrected back to read *formation,* as originally intended" (ibid).
    *   "Many other spelling errors appear to have been strictly typographical for example, *aaswer, amog, bacause, daghter, mnltitude, theit,* and *uttered*" (ibid).

    Here is a partial list of changes:

    *   *which* to *who* 891 times
    *   *was* to *were* 162 times
    *   *that* was deleted 188 times
    *   *is* to *are* 74 times
    *   *done* to *did* 10 times
    *   *straight* to *strait* 10 times
    *   *exceeding* to *exceedingly* 177 times
    *   *the* was deleted 48 times
    *   *it came to pass* was deleted 46 times
    *   *a* and *an* were deleted 40 times
    *   *had* was deleted 29 times
    *   Thousands of errors occurred with phonetic spellings: *adhear, adultry, babtized, befal, burthensome, centre, condescention, devlish, fraid, phrensied,* and *sepulcher.* Phonetic spellings were common during the time of the translation.

- In Mosiah 21:28 and Ether 4:1, the first edition had "Benjamin" where the name of Mosiah now appears. It seems that King Benjamin would not likely have still been living in the historical period described by these verses. In the 1837 edition, the Prophet Joseph made this correction.
- "In a few places, however, Joseph Smith did intentionally add to the text to clarify a point. An illustration of this is the added words *the son of* in 1 Nephi 11:21, 32, and 13:40. The text would be correct with or without the additional words, but the addition helps the reader avoid misunderstanding" (https://www.churchofjesuschrist.org/study/ensign/1983/12/understanding-textual-changes-in-the-book-of-mormon?lang=eng).
- "In 2 Nephi 30:6, *white* appeared in the 1830 and 1837 editions. Joseph changed this word to *pure* in the 1840 edition. But later American editions did not show this change because they had followed the first European and 1837 editions. This correction by the Prophet has finally been restored in the 1981 edition" (ibid).
- Alma 41:1 in the 1830 edition read, "some have arrested the scriptures," which of course now reads, "some have wrested the scriptures" (https://journal.interpreterfoundation.org/the-pleading-bar-of-god).

Dr. Skousen has documented another change that may appear in a future edition of the Book of Mormon. I am sure it would require the prophet's concurrence. The last verse in our current edition reads: "And now I bid unto all, farewell. I soon go to rest in the paradise of God, until my spirit and body shall again reunite, and I am brought forth triumphant through the air, to meet you before the pleasing bar of the great Jehovah, the Eternal Judge of both quick and dead. Amen" (Moroni 10:34). Dr. Skousen has found evidence that *pleasing* should be *pleading,* which dramatically changes the meaning.

In the end, it is not about thousands of changes. It is about the witness of the Holy Ghost that the Book of Mormon is true.

All this and more in 65 working days.

Evidence 9
Nahom

A TESTIMONY DOESN'T HINGE ON physical evidences, but they are nice bonuses. Who would have thought that the time and place of Ishmael's death would establish a future evidence of the Book of Mormon? The text reads, "And it came to pass that Ishmael died, and was buried in the place which was called Nahom" (1 Nephi 16:34). Ishmael's burial place both names and pinpoints a physical location. Nahom is only mentioned this one time in all scripture.

Vowels in Hebrew are spoken but not written. *Nahom* in English is *NHM* in Hebrew. Strikingly, altars dating from the time of Lehi have been found with the inscription "NHM" (www.fairlatterdaysaints.org/answers/Book_of_Mormon/Geography/Old_World/Nahom#The_description_of_Lehi.27s_desert_journey_matches_exactly_how_one_would_traverse_Arabia). These three altars in Jawf Valley in Yemen date from the approximate time Lehi's group would have been in the area. Nephi's party reached an area "which was called Nahom" (1 Nephi 16:34) near the time that they make an eastward turn in their journey.

NHM (the root for naham) appears twenty-five times in the narrative books [about] the Bible, and in every case it is associated with death. It is logical that Nephi would mention the distraught response of Ishmael's daughters to their father's death. We feel for Ishmael's daughters who "did mourn exceedingly, because of the loss of their father, and because of their afflictions in the wilderness; and they did murmur against [Lehi], because he had brought them out of the land of Jerusalem, saying: Our father is dead; yea, and we have wandered much in the wilderness, and we have suffered much affliction, hunger, thirst, and fatigue; and after all these sufferings we must perish in the wilderness with hunger . . . and they were desirous to return again to Jerusalem" (1 Nephi 16:35–36). Even in the most ideal circumstances, which these were not, having a parent pass away is hard. But perhaps Ishmael's daughters could have gained a little comfort had they known God's great purpose in identifying Nahom—to provide evidence to future generations of the truthfulness of the Book of Mormon.

Researchers have noted an old Hebrew mourning custom of the desert in which "the young women of the nomad tribes mourn at the grave, around which they dance singing lightly." When a man dies, "his wives, daughters, and female relations unite in cries of lamentation (weloulouá), which they repeat several times. . . . As is well known, no traditions are more unchanging through the centuries than funerary customs.

"Joseph Smith could have known almost nothing about ancient Arabia when he began translating the Book of Mormon. Yet the narrative of the journey of the party of Lehi and Sariah through ancient Arabia, written by their son Nephi, fits with what we know about the Arabian Peninsula. . . . In the view of one recent commentator, the discovery of the altars amounts to 'the first actual archaeological evidence for the historicity of the Book of Mormon'" (www.fairlatterdaysaints.org/answers/Book_of_Mormon/Geography/Old_World/Nahom#The_description_of_Lehi.27s_desert_journey_matches_exactly_how_one_would_traverse_Arabia).

"Such discoveries demonstrate as firmly as possible by archaeological means the existence of the tribal name NHM in that part of Arabia in the seventh and sixth centuries BC, the general dates assigned to the carving of the altars by the excavators. In the view of one recent commentator, the discovery of the altars amounts to 'the first actual archaeological evidence for the historicity of the Book of Mormon'" (Terryl L. Givens, *By the Hand of Mormon: The American Scripture That Launched a New World Religion* [New York: Oxford Univ. Press, 2002], 120).

Nahom. Another evidence of something Joseph got right without knowing there was anything to get right!

And all this and more in 65 working days.

Evidence 10
Joseph Finds Himself in the Text

THIS CHAPTER IS NOT ACTUAL evidence and would be better titled "An Interesting Sidenote: Joseph Finds Himself in the Text." I include it here to show Joseph's foreordination.

Joseph and Oliver worked day after day on the Book of Mormon. No doubt, the storyline captured their attention, but there were times in the dictation process when Joseph read information that specifically pertained to him. These moments must have been surprising and validating. I would have loved to be a silent observer of Joseph's reactions. Here are three examples.

In the first several chapters of 2 Nephi, Lehi gives blessings to his children, realizing his time on Earth is coming to an end. In Lehi's blessing to his youngest son, Joseph, Lehi speaks of four different men named Joseph.

1.   The first Joseph is Lehi's son, his "last-born, whom I have brought out of the wilderness of mine afflictions" (2 Nephi 3:3). The second Joseph is Joseph of Egypt of whom Lehi is a descendant: "I am a descendant of Joseph who was carried captive into Egypt" (2 Nephi 3:4). Lehi then quotes a prophecy given by Joseph of Egypt: "Thus saith the Lord unto me: A choice seer will I raise up out of the fruit of thy loins; and he shall be esteemed highly among the fruit of thy loins. And unto him will I give commandment that he shall do a work for the fruit of thy loins, his brethren, which shall be of great worth unto them, even to the bringing of them to the knowledge of the covenants which I have made with thy fathers. . . . And his name shall be called after me; and it shall be after the name of his father" (2 Nephi 3:7, 15). Four Josephs: Joseph, Lehi's son; Joseph of Egypt; Joseph, a choice seer; Joseph, the choice seer's father.

While translating an ancient document, written some two thousand years before his birth, Joseph Smith found a prophecy about himself and his father.

I wonder at what point Joseph recognized that he was reading about himself. It is also interesting to note that Joseph and Lucy Smith did not name their *first* son after his father, but their third.

2.   Nine chapters into the Book of Mormon, Joseph found something exceptionally significant when Nephi spoke of the different plates he was making. Circa 596 BC, Nephi wrote: "I have received a commandment of the Lord that I should make these plates, for the special purpose that there should be an account engraven of the ministry of my people. . . . The Lord hath commanded me to make these plates for a *wise purpose* in him, which purpose I know not" (1 Nephi 9:3, 5, italics added). Elder Holland said: "At least six times in the Book of Mormon, the phrase 'for a wise purpose' is used in reference to the making, writing, and preserving of the small plates of Nephi (see 1 Nephi 9:5; Words of Mormon 1:7; Alma 37:2, 12, 14, 18). We know one such wise purpose—the most obvious one—was to compensate for the future loss of 116 pages of manuscript translated by the Prophet Joseph Smith from the first part of the Book of Mormon (see D&C 3, 10)" (https://www. churchofjesuschrist.org/study/ensign/1996/01/for-a-wise-purpose?lang=eng).

You probably know that Martin Harris was Joseph's scribe for most of those first 116 pages. It was June of 1828. Lucy Harris, Martin's wife, was unhappy about the time Martin was spending with Joseph. She thought his time would be better spent on the farm. She also complained when Martin gave Joseph money. To pacify Lucy, Martin asked for permission to take the manuscript home. After consulting with the Lord and being told "no" twice, Joseph asked again. This time, the Lord gave a conditional "okay," requiring Martin agree to show them only to certain family members, and Joseph reluctantly allowed Martin to borrow the 116 pages of the original Book of Mormon manuscript. Sadly, the manuscript went missing and has never been found.

About a year later, Joseph and Oliver were working on the Book of Mormon. Joseph read to Oliver: "And now, as I have spoken concerning these plates, behold they are not the plates upon which I make a full account of the history of my people. . . . I have received a commandment of the Lord that I should make these plates, *for the special purpose* that there should be an account engraven of the ministry of my people. Upon the other plates should be engraven an account of the reign of the kings, and the wars and contentions of my people; wherefore these plates are for the more part of the ministry. . . . But the Lord knoweth all things from the beginning; wherefore, *he prepareth a way* to accomplish all his works among the children of men; for behold, he hath all power unto the fulfilling of all his words" (1 Nephi 9:2–6).

In June 1828, when the 116 manuscript pages went missing, Joseph did not know the Lord had provided a backup. So when Joseph learned that the manuscript was gone, he gave way to despair, crying out in agony: "All is lost! all is lost!" (https://www.josephsmithpapers.org/paper-summary/lucy-mack-smith-history-1845/138). As a consequence, Moroni took back the Urim and Thummim, and Joseph did not resume translating for about nine months. Later, when Oliver and Joseph had nearly completed the record, Joseph asked the Lord if he should retranslate the 116 lost pages. The Lord gave an emphatic no and said that "Satan hath put it into their [those who stole the manuscript] hearts to alter the words. . . . I will not suffer that Satan shall accomplish his evil design" (Doctrine and Covenants 10:10, 14).

3.   On another occasion, Joseph and Oliver are working through the book of Ether.

Joseph is reading the words of Moroni, who is abridging the Jaredite record, when Moroni seems to speak to the future translator of the record, addressing him as "you." Remember that Joseph and Moroni have met face to face many times. Moroni tells Joseph two important things.

- First: "I, Moroni . . . have told you the things which I have sealed up; therefore touch them not in order that ye may translate; for that thing is forbidden you, except by and by it shall be wisdom in God" (Ether 5:1).
- Second: "And behold, ye may be privileged that ye may show the plates unto those who shall assist to bring forth this work; And unto three shall they be shown by the power of God; wherefore they shall know of a surety that these things are true. And in the mouth of three witnesses shall these things be established; and the testimony of three, and this work, in the which shall be shown forth the power of God and also his word, of which the Father, and the Son, and the Holy Ghost bear record—and all this shall stand as a testimony against the world at the last day" (Ether 5:2–4).

Revelation upon revelation, truth upon truth. And all this and more in 65 working days.

Evidence 11
Three Official Witnesses

EVIDENCES 11, 12, AND 13 detail another aspect of the 65-day miracle. In this short period of time, men and women of integrity stepped forward to help Joseph with the work of bringing forth the Book of Mormon. The hand of God is seen as men and women risk their reputations by supporting Joseph. The testimonies of Three, Eight, and some unofficial witnesses buoyed Joseph and provided a latticework of strength on which the Church grew.

Allow me to introduce you to the three official witnesses of the Book of Mormon: Oliver Cowdery, David Whitmer, Martin Harris. Their testimony is found in the introductory pages of the Book of Mormon. These firsthand witnesses suffered persecutions ranging from intimidation to life-threatening violence and stayed true to their testimonies till death.

Oliver Cowdery was Joseph's primary scribe. He was a schoolteacher in Palmyra and boarded with Joseph's parents, where he learned about Joseph's visions and the gold plates. Oliver, with a little help from other scribes, wrote the original Book of Mormon manuscript and then, at Joseph's request, made a second copy known as the printer's manuscript. It is estimated that Oliver wrote the Book of Mormon 1.85 times. Oliver was with Joseph when John the Baptist appeared, ordained them to the Aaronic Priesthood, and instructed them to baptize each other. Joseph baptized Oliver; then Oliver baptized the Prophet. Oliver received the Melchizedek Priesthood under the hands of Peter, James, and John. He also was with Joseph in the Kirtland Temple when Jesus Christ, Moses, Elijah, and Elias appeared.

Martin Harris was a prosperous farmer acquainted with the Smith family. He was Joseph's scribe for the first 116 pages of the Book of Mormon translation. Aside from being one of the Three Witnesses, the singular accomplishment that will forever be his legacy is his mortgaging part of his farm to pay for the printing of the first edition of the Book of Mormon.

David Whitmer likewise played a pivotal role in the translation of the plates. In June 1829, he received a personal revelation now known as Doctrine and Covenants 14. Verses 8 and 11 read: "And it shall come to pass, that if you shall ask the Father in my name, in faith believing, you shall receive the Holy Ghost, which giveth utterance, that you may stand as a witness of the things of which you shall both hear and see. . . . And behold, thou art David, and thou art called to assist; which thing if ye do, and are faithful, ye shall be blessed both spiritually and temporally, and great shall be your reward." When persecution threatened the work of translation in Harmony, Pennsylvania, Oliver wrote to his friend David and asked if he and Joseph could live at David's home in Fayette, New York. David was able to persuade his parents, Peter and Mary, and went to Harmony to help Joseph and Oliver move. Joseph and Oliver lived at the Whitmer home until the translation was complete. David was one of the original six members of the Church.

The process of these three men becoming the principal witnesses to the Book of Mormon is interesting. When Martin Harris first met Oliver Cowdery and David Whitmer, who were already friends, the three united in a desire to help bring forth the Book of Mormon. At some point, the idea that they could be the three witnesses became their combined yearning. The fact that there would be three special witnesses is mentioned in the Book of Mormon three times. 2 Nephi 11:3: "Wherefore, by the words of three, God hath said, I will establish my word." 2 Nephi 27:12: "Three witnesses shall behold it, by the power of God . . . and they shall testify to the truth of the book and the things therein." Ether 5:3: "Unto three shall they be shown by the power of God; wherefore they shall know of a surety that these things are true."

Martin, Oliver, and David asked Joseph to enquire of the Lord if they might be these three witnesses. In response, the Lord explained that the three were volunteering for a lifelong commitment and responsibility, far beyond what they could have foreseen. To the Three Witnesses the Lord said: "Behold, I say unto you, that you must rely upon my word, which if you do with full purpose of heart, you shall have a view of the plates, and also of the breastplate, the sword of Laban, the Urim and Thummim, which were given to the brother of Jared upon the mount, when he talked with the Lord face to face, and the miraculous directors which were given to Lehi while in the wilderness on the borders of the Red Sea" (D&C 17:1). It is an added testimony that the three witnesses were to testify of more than just the plates. Their testimony included the plates, the breastplate, the sword of Laban, the Urim and Thummim, and the directors (the Liahona).

The Lord continued his instructions: "It is by your faith that you shall obtain a view of them, even by that faith which was had by the prophets of old. And after that you have obtained faith, and have seen them with your eyes, you shall testify of them, by the power of God" (D&C 17:2–3).

Then the Lord plainly explained why witnesses were necessary: "And this you shall do that my servant Joseph Smith, Jun., may not be destroyed, that I may bring about my righteous purposes unto the children of men in this work" (D&C 17:4). The weightiest of burdens rested on these three men's minds, hearts, and souls.

The History of the Church details: "On a summer day in 1829, Joseph Smith, Oliver Cowdery, David Whitmer, and Martin Harris went into the woods near the Whitmer home to prepare to see the gold plates. They knelt in prayer and each took a turn praying, but they received no answer. They each prayed again, but still there was no answer. Martin Harris felt that they were not receiving an answer because of some things he had done, so he left the group. The others again knelt in prayer, and soon a light appeared above them and the angel Moroni stood before them. Moroni held the gold plates in his hands and turned the plates one by one so the men could see the engravings on them. Then the voice of the Lord said to them, 'These plates have been revealed by the power of God, and they have been translated by the power of God. The translation of them which you have seen is correct, and I command you to bear record of what you now see and hear'" (https://doctrineandcovenantscentral.org/historical-context/dc-17/#:~:text="We%20could%20see%20them%2C",you%20now%20see%20and%20hear."). Following this miraculous experience, Joseph found Martin, and together they prayed. Again Moroni appeared and then revealed the same things to Martin.

Doctrine and Covenants 5:11–14 conveys the blessing of having three witnesses: "And in addition to your testimony, the testimony of three of my servants, whom I shall call and ordain, unto whom I will show these things, and they shall go forth with my words that are given through you. Yea, they shall know of a surety that these things are true, for from heaven will I declare it unto them. I will give them power that they may behold and view these things as they are; and to none else will I grant this power, to receive this same testimony among this generation, in this the beginning of the rising up and the coming forth of my church out of the wilderness—clear as the moon and fair as the sun, and terrible as an army with banners."

Lucy Mack Smith, Joseph's mother, wrote of how Joseph felt when he returned to the house after Moroni had showed the plates to the Three Witnesses. "They returned to the house. It was between three and four o'clock. Mrs. Whitmer and Mr. Smith and myself were sitting in a bedroom. I sat on the bedside. When Joseph came in he threw himself down beside me: 'Father! Mother!' said he, 'you do not know how happy I am. The Lord has caused the plates to be shown to three more besides me, who have also seen an angel and will have to testify to the truth of what I have said. For they know for themselves that I do not go about to deceive the people. And I do feel as though I was relieved of a dreadful burden, which was almost too much for me to endure. But they will now have to bear a part, and it does rejoice my soul that I am not any longer to be entirely alone in the world.' Martin Harris then came in. He seemed almost overcome with excess joy. He then testified to what he had seen and heard, as did also others, Oliver and David. Their testimony was the same in substance as that contained in the Book of Mormon" (Lucy Smith, preliminary manuscript of *Biographical Sketches*, also cited in *Biographical Sketches*, 139. Cited in Richard Lloyd Anderson, *Investigating the Book of Mormon Witnesses* [1981], 14).

Joseph Smith knew how essential the Three Witnesses were to building the kingdom: "The kingdom of heaven is like unto leaven which a woman took and hid in three measures of meal, until the whole was leavened. It may be understood that the church of the Latter Day Saints, has taken its rise from a little leaven that was put into three witnesses. Behold how much this is like the parable; it is fast leavening the lump, and will soon leaven the whole" (Letter to the Elders of the Church, 30 November–1 December 1835; online at josephsmithpapers.org).

All this and more in 65 working days.

Evidence 12
Eight Official Witnesses

ALLOW ME TO INTRODUCE YOU to the eight official witnesses who held the plates in their hands: Christian Whitmer; Jacob Whitmer; Peter Whitmer, Junior; John Whitmer; Hiram Page; Joseph Smith, Senior; Hyrum Smith; and Samuel H. Smith. These Eight Witnesses were essential to building the kingdom, but in different ways. Of the eight, only the three Smiths stayed faithful to their testimonies and to the Church after Joseph's martyrdom. (Christian Whitmer and Peter Whitmer Jr. died in 1835 and 1836. They died in full fellowship.)

Joseph Smith Sr. was baptized on April 7, 1830, a day after the organization of the Church. He had no difficulty believing Joseph's stories of angels and visions because he had received his own remarkable spiritual experiences (https://www.ldsliving.com/4-prophetic-and-beautiful-dreams-from-joseph-smiths-parents/s/91423). When he was sixty-four, he served a mission with his brother John. They traveled nearly 2,400 miles, sharing the gospel and giving patriarchal blessings. On his deathbed, he promised his son Joseph, "You shall even live to finish your work." According to Lucy Mack Smith, Joseph Jr. "cried out, weeping, 'Oh, my father, will I?' 'Yes,' said his father, 'you shall live to lay out the plan of all the work which God has given you to do. This is my dying blessing upon your head in the name of Jesus'" (www.churchofjesuschrist.org/study/manual/teachings-joseph-smith/chapter-14?lang=eng).

Hyrum Smith, Joseph's older brother, was a faithful supporter of the Prophet and seer. After his father died, Hyrum became patriarch to the Church. He died a martyr's death with Joseph in Carthage Jail. Of him, Joseph said: "Brother Hyrum, what a faithful heart you have got! Oh, may the Eternal Jehovah crown eternal blessings upon your head, as a reward for the care you have had for my soul! Oh, how many are the sorrows we have shared together; and again we find ourselves shackled with the unrelenting hand of oppression.

Hyrum, thy name shall be written in the Book of the Law of the Lord, for those who come after thee to look upon, that they may pattern after thy works" (www.churchofjesuschrist.org/study/manual/teachings-joseph-smith/ chapter-40?lang=eng).

Samuel Harrison Smith, Joseph's younger brother, was the third person baptized into the Church, one of six founding members, and the first missionary of the restored Church. He gave copies of the Book of Mormon to Phineas Young and John P. Green, who shared the book with Heber C. Kimball and Brigham Young. Samuel was chased by the mob on the day his brothers Joseph and Hyrum were martyred, receiving an internal injury that took his life thirty-three days later. His obituary stated: "If ever there lived a good man upon the earth, Samuel H. Smith was that person" (*HC 7.222*).

The other five of the Eight Witnesses, the four Whitmers and Hiram Page, (brother-in-law of the Whitmers), all stayed true to the fact that they saw the plates, held the plates, and turned the leaves. They were key players in the building of the kingdom of God on Earth. In 1838, the living members of Whitmer family became estranged from Joseph in a leadership misunderstanding in Far West, Missouri. They were excommunicated along with other dissenters. None of them reconnected with the Church in this life. (As mentioned, Christian Whitmer died in 1835 and Peter Jr. in 1836.)

Hiram Page left this powerful testimony as a disaffected member: "As to the book of Mormon, it would be doing injustice to myself, and to the work of God in the last days, to say that I could know a thing to be true in 1830, and know the same thing to be false in 1847. To say that a man of Joseph's ability, who at that time did not know how to pronounce the word Nephi, could write a book of six hundred pages, as correct as the book of Mormon, without super natural power . . . yeah, it would be treating the God of heaven with contempt to deny these testimonies, with too many others to mention here" (Letter of Hiram Page to William E. McLellin, May 30, 1847, Ray County, Missouri, cited in *Ensign of Liberty* 1 [1848]: 63).

Hiram's family also acknowledged his place in history as one of the Eight Witnesses on his headstone, which read "Hiram Page one of the eight witnesses to the Book of Mormon" https://www.thechurchnews.com/2001/1/6/23245082/ hiram-pages-grave-identified).

These Eight Witnesses deserve our appreciation and thanks. As Joseph described the Three Witnesses as being leaven, so also did these eight help leaven the whole.

All this and more in 65 working days.

Unofficial Witnesses

JOSEPH WAS BLESSED TO SHARE the burden of testimony with eleven official witnesses. Others were unofficial witnesses. Here are the witnesses of his wife, his mother, two of his siblings, Mary Musselman Whitmer, and Peter Senior.

Emma Smith, Joseph's Wife

Joseph's wife, Emma, interacted with the plates on numerous occasions. She accompanied Joseph to the Hill Cumorah the night he received the plates. Once home, she gave him a table linen to cover the plates. She moved them and dusted around them. She said, "I once felt of the plates as they thus lay on the table, tracing their outline and shape. They seemed to be pliable like thick paper, and would rustle with a metallic sound when the edges were moved by the thumb, as one does sometimes thumb the edges of a book" (https://knowhy.bookofmormoncentral.org/knowhy/how-did-emma-smith-help-bring-forth-the-book-of-mormon). She was Joseph's first scribe and supported him when persecution forced them to move several times to complete the translation. She suffered along with him and watched his abusers chase him, threaten him, accost him, tar and feather him, file court proceedings against him, and jail him. Her actions speak volumes. (See https://www.churchofjesuschrist.org/study/ensign/1979/09/the-elect-lady-emma-hale-smith?lang=eng).

Near the end of her life, Emma told her son, Joseph Smith III: "My belief is that the Book of Mormon is of divine authenticity—I have not the slightest doubt of it. I am satisfied that no man could have dictated the writing of the manuscripts unless he was inspired; for, when acting as his scribe, your father would dictate to me hour after hour; and when returning after meals, or after interruptions, he would at once begin where he had left off, without either seeing the manuscript or having any portion of it read to him. This was a usual thing for him to do. It would have been improbable that a learned man could do this; and, for one so ignorant and unlearned as he was, it was simply impossible" (https://www.fairlatterdaysaints.org/answers/Source:Last_Testimony_of_Sister_Emma).

Lucy Mack Smith, Joseph's Mother

Lucy Mack Smith wrote *The History of Joseph Smith by His Mother*. In Evidence 3, you read her memories of Joseph showing her the breastplate. In Evidence 10, you read her account of Joseph coming home after Moroni had shown the Three Witnesses the plates. In her book, she wrote about a confrontation she had with a reverend.

When Reverend Ruggles was introduced to Lucy, he asked: "Are you the mother of that poor, foolish, silly boy, Joe Smith, who pretended to translate the Book of Mormon?"

"I am, sir, the mother of Joseph Smith, but why do you apply to him such epithets as those?"

"Because," said Reverend Ruggles, "that he should imagine he was going to break down all other churches with that simple 'Mormon' book."

"Did you ever read that book?" Lucy asked.

"No, it is beneath my notice," he retorted.

Said Lucy, "That book contains the everlasting gospel . . . and was written for the salvation of your soul, by the gift and power of the Holy Ghost.

"Pooh," scoffed Ruggles, "nonsense. I am not afraid of any member of my church being led astray by such stuff; they have too much intelligence."

Lucy prophesied: "Now, Mr. Ruggles, mark my words—as true as God lives, before three years we will have more than one-third of your church; and sir, whether you believe it or not, we will take the very deacon, too!" Two months later, Jared Carter was sent on a mission to Michigan. Seventy people from Reverend Ruggles church were converted, including the deacon" (Revised and Enhanced History of Joseph Smith by His Mother, Bookcraft, Lucy Mack Smith (Author), Preston Nibley (Author), Scot Facer Proctor (Editor), Maurine Jensen Proctor (Editor) 1996, 292).

On another occasion, Lucy was on a boat heading to Kirtland, Ohio. A man called to her from the shore asking: "Is the Book of Mormon true?" She said, "That book was brought forth by the power of God and translated by the same power, and if I could make my voice sound as loud as the trumpet of Michael, the archangel, I would declare the truth from land to land and from sea to sea, and echo it from isle to isle, until everyone of the whole family of man was left without excuse—for all should hear the truth of the gospel of the Son of God" (*HOJSBHM*, 268).

William and Katharine, Joseph's siblings

William wrote: "I was permitted to lift [the plates] as they lay in a pillow case; but not to see them, as it was contrary to the commands [Joseph] had received. They weighed about sixty pounds according to my best judgment. They were not quite as large as this Bible. . . . One could easily tell that they were not stone, hewn out to deceive, or even a block of wood. . . . [T]hey were much heavier than stone and very much heavier than wood" (Richard Lloyd Anderson, *Investigating the Book of Mormon Witnesses* [Salt Lake City: Deseret Book Co., 1981], 22–23). Later in his life, William said, "I could tell they were plates of some kind and that they were fastened together by rings running through the back" (ibid., 24).

Katharine told that "Joseph allowed her to 'heft' the package but not to see the gold plates, as the angel had forbidden him to show them at that period. She said they were very heavy" (Richard Lloyd Anderson, *Investigating the Book of Mormon Witnesses* [Salt Lake City: Deseret Book Co., 1981], 22–23). Katharine's spiritual testimony of reading the Book of Mormon is persuasive: "Many times when I have read its sacred pages, I have wept like a child, while the Spirit has borne witness with my spirit to its truth" (ibid., 26).

Mary Musselman Whitmer

Mary Musselman Whitmer, wife of Peter Whitmer, Senior, was exhausted by her household tasks while hosting Joseph, Emma, and Oliver in their home. Her experience with Moroni, previously mentioned in Evidence 11, is quoted here by her son John: "One night after working all day, I went out to the barn to milk the cows. There I met a stranger. He had something on his back that looked like a knapsack. At first I was a little afraid, but then he spoke in a kind and friendly voice that put me right at ease. The man talked about the nature of the work that was going on in my house, and it filled me with such inexpressible joy and satisfaction. He unwrapped the knapsack and showed me a bundle of plates. He turned each of the golden leaves one-by-one and showed me the engravings written upon them. Then he told me to suffer my burdens for just a little while longer and that I would be blessed if I just stood faithful to the end. Then the stranger disappeared suddenly, and I could not tell where he had gone. From that moment my burdens became lighter, and I had no more desire to murmur or complain" (John C. Whitmer, interview with Andrew Jenson and Edward Stevenson 11 Oct. 1888, in *Volume 5* (2003), 261–63).

Peter Whitmer Senior

Peter Senior, along with Mary, provided food, shelter, and safety in their log home where 30 percent of the Book of Mormon translation was completed. On April 6, 1830, the Church of Jesus Christ was officially organized in the Whitmer home. Many revelations were received in or near the Whitmer home between June 1829 and January 1831: Doctrine and Covenants 14-18, 20-21, 28-31, 33-36, 38-40.

All this and more in 65 working days.

Evidence 14
Versions of the First Vision

JOSEPH'S ENEMIES WOULD HAVE YOU believe that the existence of multiple accounts of the First Vision is a testimony breaker. I am positive that if there were only one account, these same adversaries would dwell on the fact that there was only one. There are ten accounts. They do not contradict each other, and each adds context when the circumstances and intended audience are factored in. Joseph wrote or dictated four of these.

In 1832, Joseph, in his own handwriting, shares what led him to the grove to pray. He said he "cried unto the Lord for mercy for there was none else to whom I could go and obtain mercy." He continued, "And the Lord heard my cry in the wilderness. . . . I was filled with the spirit of God and the Lord opened the heavens upon me and I saw the Lord and He spake unto me saying, 'Joseph, my son, thy sins are forgiven thee'" (https://www.josephsmithpapers.org/paper-summary/history-circa-summer-1832/3).

In the 1835 account, Joseph speaks of James 1:5 as a motivation to pray. He wrote: "Information was what I most desired at this time, and with a fixed determination to obtain it . . . I made a fruitless attempt to pray; my tongue seemed to be swollen in my mouth, so that I could not utter. I heard a noise behind me, like some person walking towards me. I strove again to pray but could not. The noise of walking seemed to draw nearer. I sprung up on my feet and looked around but saw no person or thing that was calculated to produce the noise of walking" (https://www.churchofjesuschrist.org/study/manual/first-vision-accounts/1835-account?lang=eng).

The 1838 account is canonized in the Pearl of Great Price as Joseph Smith—History. This version emphasizes his desire to know which church is right and the intense opposition he experienced. It historically documents "the rise and progress of the Church" (Joseph Smith-History 1:1).

The 1842 account, known as the Wentworth Letter, highlights the differences between The Church of Jesus Christ of Latter-day Saints and other sects of the day.

> When about fourteen years of age, I began to reflect upon the importance of being prepared for a future state, and upon enquiring about the plan of salvation, I found that there was a great clash in religious sentiment; if I went to one society, they referred me to one plan, and another to another, each one pointing to his own particular creed as the summum bonum of perfection. Considering that all could not be right, and that God could not be the author of so much confusion, I determined to investigate the subject more fully, believing that if God had a church it would not be split up into factions, and that if he taught one society to worship one way, and administer in one set of ordinances, he would not teach another principles which were diametrically opposed. Believing the word of God, I had confidence in the declaration of James: "If any man lack wisdom, let him ask of God, who giveth to all men liberally and upbraideth not, and it shall be given him." (https://www.churchofjesuschrist.org/study/manual/first-vision-accounts/1842-account?lang=eng)

Until a 2019 BYU devotional address by Elder Gary E. Stevenson, I knew of six secondhand accounts of the First Vision written by Orson Pratt, Orson Hyde, Levi Richards, David Nye White, Alexander Neibaur, and Charles Walker. But Elder Stevenson related how his fifth great-grandfather Edward Stevenson, at age thirteen, heard the Prophet speak in a schoolhouse in Pontiac, Michigan. Grandpa Stevenson wrote: "I can very well remember many of the words of the boy Prophet as they were uttered in simplicity, but with a power which was irresistible to all present. . . . Here are some of the Prophet's words. With uplifted hand he said: 'I am a witness that there is a God, for I saw Him in open day, while praying in a silent grove, in the spring of 1820. He further testified that God, the Eternal Father, pointing to a separate personage, in the likeness of Himself, said: 'This is my Beloved Son hear ye Him.' O how these words thrilled my entire system and filled me with joy unspeakable to behold one who, like Paul the apostle of olden time, could with boldness testify that he had been in the presence of Jesus Christ!" (Gary E. Stevenson, "The Ongoing Restoration," Brigham Young University Campus Education Week address, August 20, 2019), speeches.byu.edu).

Perhaps this account was unknown at the time a video was produced for the Church History Museum in Salt Lake City using first- and secondhand accounts of the First Vision. In the museum is a small theater with a 240-degree screen. There, a seven-minute video, "Ask of God" plays in seven languages. The video is beautiful. You can also watch it online: (https://www.churchofjesuschrist.org/media/video/2017-01-0100-ask-of-god-joseph-smiths-first-vision?lang=eng).

Below is the text of the first three paragraphs of the video. The text is dotted with footnotes, indicating in which of the First Vision accounts each particular statement is found. As you read, you will feel the spiritual power of the words. On any given day when I am in the museum as a docent, I watch this video at least once, and sometimes four or five times with museum visitors. I never tire of it. The thought often comes to my mind, "Praise to the man who communed with Jehovah," (W. W. Phelps, *Hymns*, no. 27).

I invite you to watch the video, and if you have questions, I refer you to https://www.josephsmithpapers.org/site/accounts-of-the-first-vision or *The Heavens Are Opened*, a publication of The Sons of the Utah Pioneers magazine, pages 34–50.

> *Joseph Smith: My name is Joseph Smith. [When I was young],
> there was in the place where we lived an unusual excitement on
> the subject of religion.[1] My mind became seriously impressed
> with regard to the welfare of my soul.[2] I pondered many things
> in my heart.[3] I felt to mourn for my own sins and the sins of the
> world.[4] [But] upon inquiring [about] the plan of salvation, I
> found that there was a great clash in religious sentiment.[5]*
>
> *This was grief to my soul.[6] I knew not who was right or who
> was wrong, and I considered it of the first importance that I
> should be right in matters that involve[d] eternal consequences.[7]
> [I] wanted to get religion, too. [I] wanted to feel and shout
> like the rest, but could feel nothing.[8] I was one day reading the*

---

1 1838
2 1832
3 1832
4 1832
5 1842
6 1832
7 1835
8 Neibaur

Epistle of James . . .[9] *"If any of you lack wisdom, let him ask of God. . . . And it shall be given him."*[10] *It seemed to enter with great force into every feeling of my heart.*[11]

After I retired into the place where I had previously designed to go, having looked around me and finding myself alone, I kneeled down and began to offer up the desires of my heart to God.[12] *I cried unto the Lord for mercy for there was none else to whom I could go [. . .] to obtain mercy.*[13] *(It was the first time in my life that I had made the attempt to pray vocally.)*[14]

Immediately, I was seized upon by some power which entirely overcame me and had such astonishing influence over me as to bind my tongue so I could not speak.[15] *[My] mind filled with doubts [and] all manner of inappropriate images.*[16] *It seemed to me for a time as if I were doomed to sudden destruction.*[17] *But exerting all my powers to call upon God to deliver me*[18] *. . . my mouth was opened and my tongue liberated.*[19]

These versions testify to me that Joseph Smith's First Vision experience was multilayered and multifaceted. I like the way Elder Kyle S. McKay, a General Authority Seventy and assistant executive director of the Church History Department said, "Historians expect that when an individual retells an experience in multiple settings to different audiences over many years, each account will emphasize various aspects of the experience and contain unique details.

"There is scriptural precedent for such variations. Consider the multiple scriptural accounts of Paul's vision on the road to Damascus and the Apostles' experience on the Mount of Transfiguration.

"Some have mistakenly argued that any variation in the retelling of the story is evidence of fabrication. To the contrary, the rich historical record

9 1838
10 James 1:5
11 1838
12 1838
13 1832
14 1838
15 1838
16 Hyde
17 1838
18 1838
19 1835

enables us to learn more about this remarkable event than we could if it were less well documented" (https://www.churchofjesuschrist.org/church/news/why-are-there-multiple-accounts-of-the-first-vision-and-what-can-we-learn-from-them?lang=eng#:~:text=Each%20of%20Joseph%27s%20four%20First,%2C"%20said%20Elder%20Kyle%20S).

All this and more in 65 working days.

Evidence 15
Reformed Egyptian Names

I HAVE ENJOYED STUDYING THE Reformed Egyptain names in the Book of Mormon. As I researched Book of Mormon names, I found a reference to a display in the Isreal Museum in Jerusalem (https://scholarsarchive.byu. edu/cgi/viewcontent.cgi?article=1239&context=jbms). Sometimes evidence for the Book of Mormon is so conclusive that it deserves a drumroll, if not fireworks. This is one. The museum display shows Hebrew seals with names engraved on them. Seals are small clay stamps that were used to verify a document. This tradition, used around the world, carries over into our culture with phrases such as "sealed with a kiss" and "signed, sealed, and delivered."

In *The Journal of Book of Mormon Studies*, John A. Tvedtnes, John Gee, and Matthew Roper published a paper about these seals: "The discovery of these Hebrew names in ancient inscriptions provides remarkable evidence for the authenticity of the Book of Mormon and provides clear refutation of those critics who would place its origin in nineteenth-century America. . . . Proper names that are attested from Hebrew inscriptions . . . [include] Sariah, Alma, Abish, Aha, Ammonihah, Chemish, Hagoth, Himni, Isabel, Jarom, Josh, Luram, Mathoni, Mathonihah, Muloki, and Sam—none of which appear in English Bibles" (ibid).

I mentioned this fact to someone whose testimony is wavering. She said, "That's easy to explain away. Joseph Smith hired a Hebrew teacher and learned Hebrew." I answered that, yes, Joseph did hire a Hebrew teacher. However, the Book of Mormon came off the press in 1830, and Joseph hired the teacher for the School of the Elders in 1836.

In total, there are 337 names in the Book of Mormon, 188 of which are unique. Scholars have validated their authenticity and shown that the Book of Mormon is indeed an ancient document. "Many Book of Mormon names are not found in the Bible, and were unknown to Joseph Smith. Yet, these names have meaning in ancient languages and/or have been found as actual names from ancient history. These 'hits' provide additional evidence that the Book of Mormon is indeed an ancient record" (https://scholarsarchive.byu. edu/cgi/viewcontent.cgi?article=1239&context=jbms). If you go to the Fair Latter-day Saint website, you will find the provenance of these names. The list includes Lehi's family excepting Jacob and Joseph, the two sons born in the wilderness, because they are Biblical names. The following are examples from the website regarding various names from Lehi's family. Some are obvious; some are technical.

- The name of LMN is found on inscriptions in the Sinai: "Greetings Lamin, son of Abdal" (Shlm Lminu bn Abdl). "Recently the name Laman (written definitely with a second "a") has turned up in south Arabia and been hailed by the discoverers as 'a new name.' In an inscription reading 'Lamai son of Nafiah erected this monument,' the final Yod is defective and suggests that the word is really Laman." (As explained in Evidence 9, vowels in Hebrew are spoken but not written, as with NHM for Nahom.)
- Lehi in the Bible is the name of a Philistine army encampment. There Samson used a donkey's jawbone and called the place Ramath Lehi which means "Jawbone Hill." Also, "A potsherd was found at Elath, where Lehi's road from Jerusalem meets 'the fountain of the Red Sea' (1 Nephi 1:9), bearing the name of a man, LHI, very clearly written on it."
- "Sariah has turned up in a papyrus document, written in Persian period Aramaic, in the era following the sixth century BC. The female Jewish/Hebrew name Sariah appears in an Aramaic papyrus from the fifth century BC (albeit partially restored by the original publisher)."
- "Nephi (BM), founder of the Nephite nation. Nehi, Nehri (OW), famous Egyptian noblemen. Nfy was the name of an Egyptian captain. Since BM insists on 'ph,' Nephi is closer to Nihpi, original name of the god Pa-nepi, which may even have been Nephi. The document . . . was found at Elephantine in upper Egypt around the year 1900."

The names in the Book of Mormon are being authenticated as new evidence is unearthed.

All this and more in 65 working days.

Prophecy

PRESIDENT JOSEPH F. SMITH WAS the first to prophecy about temples "dotting the land" (https://www.churchofjesuschrist.org/church/news/dotting-the-earth-entering-an-era-of-new-international-temples?lang=eng). I remember when President Spencer W. Kimball announced the temple in Tokyo, Japan, in 1975. I thought, "Temples are surely dotting the land." I thought the same thing when President Gordon B. Hinckley announced the rebuilding of the Nauvoo Temple in 1999. At this writing, President Russell M. Nelson has announced 153 temples. (I have chosen a place in my neighborhood for a future temple I hope will be built there someday.) Are prophets finished announcing temples? Probably not. Is the prophecy that temples will dot the earth fulfilled? As with many prophecies, this one is being fulfilled in gradual stages. In contrast, other prophecies are fulfilled in a single event, such as the birth of Jesus Christ.

The Book of Mormon is a book of prophecy intricately woven into a narrative. Some prophecies were given and fulfilled in the thousand-year timeline of Nephite history and the perhaps 2,500 years of Jaredite history. Others have been and will yet be fulfilled for long beyond the publication of the Book of Mormon.

The first prophecy in the Book of Mormon is on page one: "In that same year there came prophets, prophesying unto the people that they must repent, or the great city of Jerusalem must be destroyed" (1 Nephi 1:4). Did the people repent? No. Was Jerusalem destroyed? Yes, in December 589 BC. "Babylon defeated the Egyptians at Carchemish in 605 B.C. Judah became a vassal of the new conquerors. Jehoiakim paid tribute to Babylon for three years before unsuccessfully attempting to free his people. The rebellious king was killed, and many of his people were exiled to Babylon. The king's wickedness had accelerated the deterioration of the people of Judah. He was succeeded by his young son Jehoiachin, who continued to resist the Babylonians but was defeated within three months" (https://www.churchofjesuschrist.org/study/manual/old-testament-student-manual-kings-malachi/enrichment-g?lang=eng).

When I realized how much prophecy was in the Book of Mormon, I wanted to know how far I would have to read to find the first one hundred. In counting them, if a prophecy was stated more than once, I only counted it the first time. Some prophecies are so complex that I did not try to capture all of the detail. In some cases, I didn't count prophecies that weren't measurable. For example, I didn't count prophecies such as, "if you keep the commandments, you will prosper in the land," or "if you don't murmur, you will be highly favored." I believe both are true, but we all experience the fulfillment of these prophecies in different ways.

Prophecy #100 is on page 52, which equals roughly two prophecies per page, and this is a cursory list. Hugh Nibley emphasized the prophetic nature of the Book of Mormon: "The Book of Mormon is a prophetic book. It was written by prophets and about prophets. It was foreseen by prophets and foresees our day. It was brought forth by prophetic gifts for prophetic purposes. It speaks in a clarion voice of warning to those who would survive the last days" (https://scholarsarchive.byu.edu/mi/88/).

The following 100 paraphrased prophecies are listed primarily for visual effect, though I would never discourage anyone from reading the list. Each is found in 1 Nephi. It's quite impressive. What is astounding is that many of them have been fulfilled.

The list of the first 100 prophecies in the Book of Mormon:

1. Jerusalem will be destroyed if the people do not repent: 1 Nephi 1:4. This is repeated many times: 1:13, 18; 2:13; 3:17; 7:13; 10:3. This prophecy was shown to be fulfilled when, in 2 Nephi 1:4, Lehi saw in vision that Jerusalem was destroyed.

2. Many people in Jerusalem will perish by the sword, and others will be carried away captive into Babylon: 1:13, 10:3.

3. A Messiah will come; He will redeem the world: 1:19.

4. Inasmuch as you keep my commandments, you will be led to a land of promise that I have prepared for you. It is choice above all others: 2:20.

5. If Laman and Lemuel rebel, they shall be cut off from the presence of the Lord: 2:21. This prophecy is fulfilled in 2 Nephi 5:20: "Wherefore,

the word of the Lord was fulfilled which he spake unto me, saying that: Inasmuch as they will not hearken unto thy words they shall be cut off from the presence of the Lord. And behold, they were cut off from his presence."

6. Nephi, if you keep the commandments, you will be a ruler and teacher over your brothers: 2:22, 3:29. Fulfilled: 2 Nephi 5:19.

7. If Laman and Lemuel rebel against God, He will curse them: 2:23.

8. If Nephites also rebel, Lamanites will be a scourge unto them: 2:24.

9. The plates of brass shall go forth unto all nations, kindreds, tongues, and people: 5:18.

10. Brass plates will not be dimmed by time: 5:19.

11. Jews will be brought back out of captivity and possess again the land of their inheritance: 10:3.

12. The Messiah will be raised up among the Jews in 600 years: 10:4.

13. A prophet will come before the Messiah to prepare the way: 10:7.

14. This prophet will baptize the Messiah with water: 10:9.

15. This prophet will bear record that he had baptized the Lamb of God who should take away the sins of the world: 10:10.

16. The gospel will be preached among the Jews: 10:11.

17. The Jews will dwindle in unbelief: 10:11.

18. The Messiah will be slain by the Jews: 10:11.

19. The Messiah will rise from the dead: 10:11.

20. The Messiah will manifest himself unto the Gentiles by the Holy Ghost: 10:11.

21. The House of Israel shall be like branches broken off and scattered upon the face of the earth: 10:12–13.

22. The House of Israel will be gathered: 10:14.

23. The Gentiles will receive the fulness of the gospel: 10:14.

24. The Gentiles will be grafted into the House of Israel and come to the knowledge of the true Messiah: 10:14.

25. If you diligently seek, the mysteries of God will be unfolded unto you by the power of the Holy Ghost: 10:19.

26. If you do wickedly and are found unclean, you will be cast off forever: 10:21.

27. Nephi saw in vision the city of Nazareth and a most beautiful virgin: 11:13.

28. Nephi saw in vision the virgin bearing a child in her arms: 11:20.

29. Nephi saw in vision the Son of God going forth among the children of men and many falling at His feet and worshipping Him: 11:24.

30. Nephi saw the Son of God baptized and the Holy Ghost abide upon Him: 11:27.

31. Nephi saw the Lamb of God preach with power and great glory and multitudes gather together to hear Him: 11:29.

32. Nephi saw twelve following the Lamb of God: 11:29.

33. Nephi saw the Lamb of God healing the sick and casting out unclean spirits: 11:31.

34. Nephi saw the Lamb of God lifted on the cross and slain for the sins of the world: 11:33.

35. Nephi saw multitudes gathered together to fight against the Apostles of the Lamb: 11:34.

36. Nephi saw the destruction of all nations, kindreds, tongues, and people the fight against the Apostles of the Lamb: 11:36.

37. Nephi saw his people multiplied greatly: 2:1.

38. Nephi saw wars and great slaughters among his people: 2:2.

39. Nephi saw darkness on the face of the land of promise—lightnings, thunderings, earthquakes, cities sunk, and others burned with fire: 12:4.

40. Nephi saw the heavens open and the Lamb of God descending out of heaven, and He showed Himself to the people who had not fallen: 12:6.

41. Nephi saw that the Holy Ghost fell upon twelve others who were ordained of God and chosen: 12:7.

42. Nephi learned the Twelve Apostles of the Lamb in Jerusalem will judge the twelve tribes of Israel: 12:9.

43. Nephi learned the Lamb would call twelve ministers who will judge His seed: 12:10.

44. Nephi saw three generations and many of the fourth pass away in righteousness following the Lamb's ministry to his people: 12:12.

45. Nephi saw the seed of his brethren contend against his seed and overpower them: 12:20.

46. Nephi saw many generations pass away and the seed of his brethren dwindle in unbelief and become a dark, loathsome, and filthy people: 12:23.

47. Nephi saw nations and kingdoms of the Gentiles form a great, abominable church: 13:4.

48. Nephi learned the devil was the founder of the great and abominable church: 13:6.

49. Nephi saw this church can be identified by silver, silks, scarlets, fine-twined linen, precious clothing, and harlots: 13:8.

50. Nephi saw the that great and abominable church destroyed the saints of God and brought them into captivity: 13:9.

51. Nephi saw many waters separate the Gentiles from the seed of his brethren: 13:10.

52. Nephi saw the wrath of God upon the seed of his brethren: 13:11.

53. Nephi saw a Gentile man wrought upon by the Spirit of God who traveled upon the many waters to the seed of his brethren in the promised land: 13:12.

54. Nephi saw other Gentiles come forth out of captivity to the promised land: 13:13.

55. Nephi saw the Gentiles scatter and smite the seed of his brethren: 13:14.

56. Nephi saw the Gentiles prosper. They were white, fair, and beautiful like his people: 13:15.

57. Nephi saw these Gentiles humble themselves, and the power of the Lord was with them: 13:16.

58. Nephi saw the mother Gentiles battle against the Gentiles in the land of promise, and the Lord delivered them out of the hands of all other nations: 13:19.

59. Nephi saw the Gentiles in the land of promise prosper, and he saw a book was carried forth among them: 13:20.

60. Nephi learned the book was similar to the brass plates and was of great worth unto the Gentiles: 13:23.

61. Nephi saw that the great and abominable church took many plain and precious parts out of the book. They also took away many covenants of the Lord to pervert the right ways of the Lord: 13:26–27.

62. Nephi saw other books come forth by the power of the Lamb to convince the Gentiles, the seed of his brethren, and the scattered Jews that the book is true: 13:39.

63. Nephi learned this last record shall make known to all kindreds, tongues, and people that the Lamb of God is the Son of the Eternal Father, and the Savior of the world; and that all men must come unto him, or they cannot be saved: 13:40.

64. Nephi saw that the first book and this last book will both establish that there is one God and one Shepherd over all the earth: 13:41.

65. Nephi saw that the Lamb will show Himself unto the Jews, and the Gentiles will be numbered among the house of Israel: 14:1–2.

66. Nephi saw the pit digged by the abominable church shall be filled by those who dug it: 14:3.

67. Nephi saw the Lamb will work a great and marvelous work among the children of men, and either they will be convinced and delivered into life eternal, or they will be brought down into captivity and destruction because there are only two churches: 14:7–10.

68. Nephi saw those who belonged to the church of the Lamb of God were few: 14:12.

69. Nephi saw the mother of abominations gather together all nations and fight against the Lamb of God: 14:13.

70. Nephi saw the members of the Lamb's church were armed with righteousness and the power of God in great glory: 14:14.

71. Nephi saw the wrath of God poured out upon that great and abominable church with wars and rumors of wars. At the same time, the work of the Father shall commence in preparing the way for His covenants to be fulfilled by the people of the house of Israel: 14:17.

72. Nephi saw one of the Apostles of the Lamb named John, whose calling was to write concerning the end of the world. Nephi was told not to write this history: 14:24–25.

73. Nephi saw that other records will come forth in purity unto the house of Israel: 14:26.

74. The fullness of the gospel of the Messiah will come to the Gentiles and from the Gentiles to Lehi's seed: 15:13.

75. Laman and Lemuel's seed will know they are of the house of Israel and that they are the covenant people of the Lord: 15:14.

76. Laman and Lemuel's posterity will come to the knowledge of their Redeemer, the very points of His doctrine, that they may know how to come unto Him and be saved: 15:14.

77. The Abrahamic covenant will be fulfilled in the latter days, through which all the kindreds of the earth be blessed: 15:18.

78. The Jews will be restored in the latter days and not be confounded or scattered again: 15:19–20.

79. Nephi is commanded to make another set of plates but doesn't know why: 19:3–6.

80. The Jews will scourge and spit on the God of Israel. He will suffer through it: 19:9.

81. The God of Abraham, Isaac, and Jacob will be crucified: 19:10.

82. The God of Israel will be buried in a sepulchre: 19:10.

83. There will be three days of darkness and great upheavals for those who live on the isles of the sea: 19:10–12.

84. When the people at Jerusalem no longer turn aside their hearts, He will gather them in from the four quarters of the earth: 19:16.

85. All the earth shall see the salvation of the Lord: 19:17.

86. The house of Israel will be scattered upon all the face of the earth, among all nations: 22:3.

87. They will harden their hearts against the Holy One of Israel and be hated of all men: 22:5.

88. The Gentiles shall nurse the house of Israel and carry their children in their arms, which is an expression of bringing the gospel to them: 22:6.

89. The Lord will raise up a mighty nation among the Gentiles, even upon the face of this nation and do a marvelous work. This is how the covenant to Father Abraham will be fulfilled that all the kindreds of the earth will be blessed to know the Lord is their Savior: 22:8–10.

90. The great and abominable church shall turn upon itself and tumble to the earth as dust, and great shall be the fall of it: 22:13–14.

91. Every nation that will war against Israel will turn against each another: 22:14.

92. The day speedily cometh when Satan will have no more power. God will not allow the wicked to destroy the righteous: 22:15–16.

93. The wicked shall be burned as stubble by the wrath of God: 22:15–16.

94. The righteous need not fear. They shall be saved, even if it so be by fire: 22:17.

95. All they who fight against Zion shall be cut off: 22:19.

96. A prophet the Lord God will raise up like unto Moses: 22:20.

97. Those who will not hear that prophet will be cut off from among the people: 22:20.

98. This prophet is the Holy One of Israel: 22:21.

99. The kingdom of the devil will be confounded: 22:22.

100. "For the time speedily shall come that all churches which are built up to get gain, and those who are built up to get power over the flesh, and those who are built up to become popular in the eyes of the world, and those who seek the lusts of the flesh and the things of the world, and to do all manner of iniquity; yea, in fine, all those who belong to the kingdom of the devil are they who need fear, and tremble, and quake; they are those who must be brought low in the dust; they are those who must be consumed as stubble; and this is according to the words of the prophet": 22:23.

All this and more in 65 working days.

Evidence 17
Covenants

"A COVENANT IS A SACRED agreement between God and His children. God sets specific conditions, and He promises to bless us as we obey these conditions. Making and keeping covenants qualifies us to receive the blessings God has promised. When we choose not to keep covenants, we cannot receive the blessings" (https://www.churchofjesuschrist.org/study/youth/learn/yw/ordinances-covenants/essential?lang=eng).

Why are covenants in the Book of Mormon evidences for the Book of Mormon? Covenants are the established pattern by which our Father in Heaven, through His Son Jesus Christ, prepares His children to return to Him. Each covenant we make and keep is like a grab bar to which we hold fast, anchoring, binding, affixing ourselves to Him. Covenants are Heavenly Father's fingerprint. If the Book of Mormon had no covenants, it would not follow scriptural pattern.

In the Old Testament, "covenant" is found 272 times. The 272nd reads: "Behold, I will send my messenger, and he shall prepare the way before me: and the Lord, whom ye seek, shall suddenly come to his temple, even the messenger of the covenant, whom ye delight in: behold, he shall come, saith the Lord of hosts" (Malachi 3:1). This use of "covenant" is also a prophecy, a prophecy that was fulfilled on April 3, 1836, in the Kirtland Temple, twenty-two centuries later. It was Easter Sunday when Jesus Christ, Moses, Elias, and Elijah appeared to Joseph Smith and Oliver Cowdery, giving them the priesthood keys necessary for the gospel to be restored in its fulness.

The Book of Mormon—the book itself—is a covenant. In 1832, the Lord said to Joseph Smith in Doctrine and Covenants 84:54–55: "Your minds in times past have been darkened because of unbelief, and because you have treated lightly the things you have received—which vanity and unbelief have brought the whole church under condemnation." This sounds serious.

What is it that has brought the whole church under condemnation? The Lord continued: "And this condemnation resteth upon the children of Zion, even all. And they shall remain under this condemnation until they repent." Repent of what? "Until they repent and remember the new covenant, even the Book of Mormon" (Doctrine and Covenants 84:56–57). The Book of Mormon is a covenant and a sign.

The Book of Mormon is a covenant and fulfills a covenant: "The coming forth of the Book of Mormon is a sign that the Lord has commenced to gather Israel and fulfill His covenants" (Headnote to 3 Nephi 29). The actual verse reads: "When the Lord shall see fit, in his wisdom, that these sayings shall come unto the Gentiles according to his word, then *ye may know that the covenant which the Father hath made with the children of Israel*, concerning their restoration to the lands of their inheritance, is already beginning to be fulfilled" (3 Nephi 29:1, italics added). Two historic dates are important in the fulfillment of this prophecy: March 26, 1830—the day the Book of Mormon was for sale in the Grandin Print Shop—and October 24, 1841—the day Orson Hyde dedicated the Holy Land for the return of the Jews.

The gospel of Jesus Christ cannot be separated from the concept of covenant. Covenants with God our Heavenly Father began with Adam and Eve in the Garden of Eden and continued through the heads of each dispensation— Enoch, Noah, Abraham, Moses, Jesus Christ, and Joseph Smith. The Book of Mormon is a covenant, fulfills a covenant, and contains covenants.

Moroni, in the next to last verse of the Book of Mormon, summarizes the meaning of covenant and shows that the Father accomplishes His work through His Son: "And again, if ye by the grace of God are perfect in Christ, and deny not his power, then are ye sanctified in Christ by the grace of God, through the shedding of the blood of Christ, which is in the covenant of the Father unto the remission of your sins, that ye become holy, without spot" (Moroni 10:33).

- I like the definition of "holy." Remember the names of Jesus Christ from Evidence 1 that begin with "holy": *Holy* Child; *Holy* God; *Holy* Messiah; *Holy* One; *Holy* One of Jacob, reiterating that He lived "without spot."
- It is meaningful that "holy" in "*Holy* Ghost is a description of what baptized and confirmed individuals may become as we hearken to His promptings. The Holy Ghost helps us keep our covenants.

Our Eternal Father and His Son jointly, in love and harmony, restored these covenants to the Prophet Joseph Smith. Acting under their authority,

Joseph directed the early Saints to build temples in which to receive and make covenants for themselves and their dead. We do the same today. Joseph also instructed and led the early Saints to fulfill their covenants by working to gather Israel and build Zion, which continues as our blessing today.

The promises Nephi and Zoram made to each other show trust, which is foundational to covenants. When Zoram tries to bolt the scene, Nephi seizes him and tells him, probably quickly, succinctly, and breathlessly, how his father was commanded by the Lord to flee Jerusalem because it was going to be destroyed, and how his father received another commandment that he and his brothers should return to Jerusalem to retrieve the plates from Laban. He then promises Zoram with an oath that if he will tarry with them in the wilderness, he will be a free man. Zoram trusts Nephi and promises to go with him and his brothers into the wilderness. And Nephi trusts Zoram's oath. "Yea, and he also made an oath unto us that he would tarry with us from that time forth. . . . When Zoram had made an oath unto us, our fears did cease concerning him" (1 Nephi 4:35, 37).

The power of covenants made and kept is based on the trustworthiness of the covenanters. In this case because of the oath, Nephi trusted Zoram, whom he had just barely met. Because of the oath, Zoram trusted Nephi, whom he had just met and who was wearing Laban's clothes. Nephi also had Zoram in a wrestling hold and three strong brothers nearby, which no doubt influenced Zoram. But once the oaths were exchanged, Nephi never had to look over his shoulder to see if Zoram was still there. An oath was an oath.

The vows between Nephi and Zoram were human to human. Covenants in scripture are between God and an individual or between God and a group of people. These covenants can be made one-on-one—as with baptism and confirmation, the sacrament, and temple covenants—or with a united voice— as when King Benjamin's people proclaimed their fidelity together: "O have mercy, and apply the atoning blood of Christ that we may receive forgiveness of our sins, and our hearts may be purified; for we believe in Jesus Christ, the Son of God, who created heaven and earth, and all things; who shall come down among the children of men" (Mosiah 4:2).

The first earthly, one-on-one covenant we make is at baptism, and the power of the baptismal covenant cannot be overstated because we renew the same covenant every time we partake of the sacrament. The covenanters are God and the person being baptized or taking the sacrament. We trust Him implicitly because we know His trustworthiness cannot be questioned. Alma, the former priest in King Noah's court, now a prophet, instructed and invited his people to be baptized. He explains that by being baptized you "witness before [God] that ye have entered into a covenant with him, that ye will serve him and keep his commandments, that he may pour out his Spirit more abundantly upon you" (Mosiah 18:10). The renewal of this covenant is sacred and a preparation for temple covenants. "According to our latter-day prophets and leaders, when you partake of the sacrament you renew whatever covenants you have made with the Lord. For example, if you have been baptized only, that is the covenant you renew" https://www.churchofjesuschrist.org/study/ensign/1995/03/i-have-a-question/i-have-a-question?lang=eng).

The blessings of covenants are evidenced in the words the Lord spoke to Alma:

"*Blessed* art thou, Alma, and *blessed* are they who were baptized in the waters of Mormon. Thou art *blessed* because of thy exceeding faith in the words alone of my servant Abinadi. And *blessed* are they because of their exceeding faith in the words alone which thou hast spoken unto them. And *blessed* art thou because thou hast established a church among this people; and they shall be established, and they shall be my people. Yea, *blessed* is this people who are willing to bear my name; for in my name shall they be called; and they are mine" (Mosiah 26:15–18). The Lord blesses Alma and his people six times in these ninety-nine words. After the blessing, He formally covenants with Alma: "Thou art my servant; and I covenant with thee that thou shalt have eternal life" (Mosiah 26:20).

All this and so much more in 65 working days.

Zion and the New Jerusalem

RECENTLY IN OUR WARD SACRAMENT meeting, I was sitting in front of two missionaries who had a young woman seated between them. The bishop welcomed the missionaries and announced the young woman was going to be baptized that very day. We sang the opening hymn, "Israel, Israel, God Is Calling." The phrase in the chorus, "Come to Zion, come to Zion," triggered a question. The young woman whispered to one of the missionaries, "What does Zion mean?" The missionary whispered back, "It is where members of the Church live." What a beautiful, simple, basic definition. The missionary could have overwhelmed her with a more technical explanation: "At various times in the Doctrine and Covenants, the word *Zion* is used to designate a physical gathering place for the Saints (the city of Zion, for example) or as an identifier of the Lord's people—'the pure in heart' [D&C 97:21]" (https://www.churchofjesuschrist.org/inspiration/what-is-zion?lang=eng).

The word "Zion" is found forty-five times in the Book of Mormon. It seems that Lehi knew the concepts of Zion when he gave his final blessing to Laman and Lemuel's posterity: "Be determined in *one mind and in one heart, united in all things*" (2 Nephi 1:21). Just as every prophet does, Lehi had hopes for Zion. He would have known how Enoch, Melchizedek, and Abraham focused on creating Zion societies and how, in many ways, they succeeded. He would have known about Moses and the rebellious children of Israel and how they had to wander forty years in the wilderness because they refused to follow the principles of Zion.

Seemingly, the pieces of the Zion puzzle were in place for Lehi to achieve his Zion goal. His society started out as a small family, free from the worldly influences of Jerusalem, and they had revelations and the Liahona to guide them. But any hopes Lehi had for a Zion society were sunk by the contention which Laman and Lemuel perpetrated. Their disappointing faithlessness pained Lehi and Sariah's hearts. Nephi said, "My parents being stricken in years, and having suffered much grief because of their children, they were brought down, yea, even upon their sick-beds. Because of their grief and much sorrow" (1 Nephi 18:17–18). If only Laman and Lemuel had been willing to follow their father, the prophet, instead of plotting to kill him, a Zion society might have been established. A community achieves Zion only when the heart of each person is pure.

The first time the word "Zion" is used in the Book of Mormon is in Nephi's tree of life vision: "And blessed are they who shall seek to bring forth my Zion at that day, for they shall have the gift and the power of the Holy Ghost; and if they endure unto the end they shall be lifted up at the last day, and shall be saved in the everlasting kingdom of the Lamb; and whoso shall publish peace, yea, tidings of great joy, how beautiful upon the mountains shall they be" (1 Nephi 13:37).

Of the 45 times "Zion" is mentioned in the Book of Mormon, 35 are found in the first two books of Nephi. Many—if not most—of these are quotes from Isaiah, the great prophet who speaks of Zion 46 times in his own book, is approximately one-third the number of times "Zion" is found in the entire Old Testament. Another clustering of the word "Zion" is spoken by Abinadi in Mosiah 12–15. Four times he speaks using Isaiah's words: "And these are they who have published peace, who have brought good tidings of good, who have published salvation; and said unto Zion: Thy God reigneth! And O how beautiful upon the mountains were their feet! And again, how beautiful upon the mountains are the feet of those that are still publishing peace! And again, how beautiful upon the mountains are the feet of those who shall hereafter publish peace, yea, from this time henceforth and forever!" (Mosiah 15:14–17).

During His time among the Nephites, Jesus Christ testifies of Isaiah's words in 3 Nephi 16, 20, and 21. Chapter 21 is especially relevant here because He teaches what "things shall be about to take place—that I shall . . . establish again among them my Zion" (3 Nephi 21:1). He very specifically warns of the cleansing that will take place: "For it shall come to pass, saith the Father, that at that day whosoever will not repent and come unto my Beloved Son, them will I cut off from among my people, O house of Israel; and I will execute vengeance and fury upon them, even as upon the heathen, such as they have not heard" (3 Nephi 21:20–21). Then He shares blessings promised in that day: "If they will repent and hearken unto my words, and harden not their hearts, I will establish my church among them, and they shall come in unto the covenant and be numbered among this the remnant of Jacob, unto whom I have given this land for their inheritance . . . that they may build a city, which shall be called the New Jerusalem. . . . And then shall the power of heaven come down among them; and I also will be in the midst" (3 Nephi 21:22–23,25).

In the same way our Savior and prophets of the past have taught and longed for Zion, our latter-day prophets teach the principles of Zion and no doubt long for such a time when we are of "one mind and in one heart, united in all things" (2 Nephi 1:21) just as Lehi said to his grandchildren.

This majestic doctrine of Zion is taught in the hymn: "Let Zion in Her Beauty Rise." When the Winter Olympics came to Salt Lake City in 2002, more than one thousand actors, singers, and dancers performed "Light of the Word—a Celebration of Life" on a domed stage in the Conference Center. I was fortunate enough to attend two rehearsals. It was moving and powerful the first time, but the second time, even more so as a new ending had been added. After ending the way it had the night before, the orchestra began to play an introduction to "Let Zion in Her Beauty Rise." Then from behind the hill on the domed stage, the Tabernacle Choir appeared, marching in rows and columns, singing only the way the Choir can. The power of the experience left me wishing I had a whole box of tissues. Zion has no equal in concept or magnitude.

> *Let Zion in her beauty rise; her light begins to shine.*
> *Ere long her King will rend the skies, majestic and divine,*
> *The gospel spreading thru the land, a people to prepare*
> *To meet the Lord and Enoch's band triumphant in the air.*
>
> *Ye heralds, sound the golden trump to earth's remotest bound.*
> *Go spread the news from pole to pole in all the nations round:*
> *That Jesus in the clouds above, with hosts of angels too,*
> *Will soon appear, his Saints to save, His enemies subdue."*
>
> *That glorious rest will then commence which prophets did foretell,*
> *When Saints will reign with Christ on earth, and in his presence*
>   *dwell*
> *A thousand years, oh, glorious day! dear Lord, prepare my heart*
> *To stand with thee on Zion's mount and nevermore to part.*
>   *(Hymns, no. 41)*

The prophets of the Book of Mormon knew about Zion. They described it, defined it, and desired it. Their information came from the brass plates. As the finale to the Book of Mormon, Moroni teaches the principles of Zion with an invitation: "And awake, and arise from the dust, O Jerusalem; yea, and put on thy beautiful garments, O daughter of Zion; and strengthen thy stakes and enlarge thy borders forever, that thou mayest no more be confounded, that the covenants of the Eternal Father which he hath made unto thee, O house of Israel, may be fulfilled" (Moroni 10:31). *If* those who seek to bring forth Zion will publish peace and endure to the end, *then* they shall be saved in the everlasting kingdom of the Lamb.

All this and more in 65 working days.

Alma 5

THE FIFTH CHAPTER OF ALMA is another powerful evidence of the miraculous coming forth of the Book of Mormon. It's just one of 236 chapters in the Book of Mormon. Doing the math, Alma 5 is about five pages long, without the footnotes, and Joseph dictated about eight pages a day. This means he spent less than a day, perhaps five hours, on Alma 5.

Alma 5 is the speech Alma gives in Zarahemla, his home town. His audience includes believers, doubters, unbelievers, and apostates.

The first thing Alma does is establish his line of authority. "I, Alma, having been consecrated by my father, Alma, to be a high priest over the church of God, he having power and authority from God . . . to establish a church [and] . . . baptize his brethren in the waters of Mormon" (Alma 5:3).

Alma's talk is filled with urgency. References to time are scattered throughout the sixty-two verses: "Could ye say, if ye were called to die at **this time**, within yourselves, that ye have been sufficiently humble?" (v. 27). "Behold ye must prepare **quickly**; for the kingdom of heaven is **soon at hand**" (v. 28). "I would that he should prepare **quickly**, for **the hour is close at hand**" (v. 29). "**The time is at hand** that he must repent or he cannot be saved!" (v. 31). "The Spirit saith . . . the King of heaven shall **very soon** shine forth among all the children of men" (v. 50). "All [they] that will persist in . . . wickedness . . . shall be hewn down and cast into the fire except they **speedily** repent" (v. 56).

Alma asks fifty questions in this one chapter. There are forty-two question marks. Here are ten of them:

- Have you sufficiently retained in remembrance the captivity of your fathers? (v. 6)
- Have you sufficiently retained in remembrance his mercy and long-suffering? (v. 6)

- Have ye sufficiently retained in remembrance that he has delivered their souls from hell? (v. 6)
- Have ye spiritually been born of God? (v. 14)
- Have ye received his image in your countenances? (v. 14)
- Have ye experienced this mighty change in your hearts? (v. 14)
- Do ye exercise faith in the redemption of him who created you? (v. 15)
- Can ye look up to God at that day with a pure heart and clean hands? (v. 19)
- Can you look up, having the image of God engraven upon your countenances? (v. 19)
- Can ye think of being saved when you have yielded yourselves to become subjects to the devil? (v. 20)

Alma Uses Comparisons and Opposing Contrasts:
captivity vs. deliverance
bondage vs. freedom
chains of hell vs. salvation
ravenous wolves vs. good shepherd
wicked vs. righteous
guilty vs. blameless
midst of darkness vs. luminated by the light
filthiness vs. purity
garments stained vs. garments cleansed
names blotted out vs. names numbered among
kingdom of the devil vs. Kingdom of God
wages of death vs. good works
bands of death vs. fruit of the tree of life
puffed up vs. humble
evil cometh from the devil vs. good cometh from God

Alma Speaks of Hearts:
- Behold, he changed their **hearts** (v. 7).
- According to [my father's faith in Abinadi's words] there was a mighty change wrought in his **heart** (v. 12).
- [My father] preached the word unto your fathers, and a mighty change was also wrought in their **hearts** (v. 13).
- Have ye experienced this mighty change in your **hearts**? (v.14).
- I say unto you, can ye look up to God at that day with a pure **heart** and clean hands? (v.19).

- If ye have experienced a change of **heart**, and if ye have felt to sing the song of redeeming love, I would ask, can ye feel so now? (v. 26).
- Can ye be puffed up in the pride of your **hearts**; yea, will ye still persist in the wearing of costly apparel and setting your hearts upon the vain things of the world, upon your riches? (v. 53).

Alma Teaches of Two Shepherds:
Behold, I say unto you, that the **good shepherd** doth call you; yea, and in his own name he doth call you, which is the name of Christ; and if ye will not hearken unto the voice of the **good shepherd**, to the name by which ye are called, behold, ye are not the sheep of the **good shepherd**. And now if ye are not the sheep of the **good shepherd**, of what fold are ye? Behold, I say unto you, that the **devil is your shepherd**. (Alma 5:38–39, emphasis added.)

Alma Gives a List of Don'ts:
• Do not trample the Holy One under your feet by laying aside His commandments.
• Do not work iniquity.
• Do not mock your brother.
• Do not heap persecutions on anyone.
• Do not be puffed up in pride.
• Do not persist in wearing costly apparel.
• Do not persist in setting your hearts on riches.
• Do not persist in supposing you are better than another.
• Do not persist in withholding your substance from individuals who are in need. (Alma 5:32–56). (It's interesting that Alma uses *persist* 5 times in 5 verses. I think he is saying, don't continue in these practices.)

It is impossible that Joseph could have composed and dictated without notes or preparation the intricacies, clarity, and artistry of this one chapter.

Character Development

Once a week I teach a Book of Mormon class on Zoom. My Relief Society president in conjunction with the bishop asked me to teach it. I thought the purpose was to give me something meaningful to do as I recovered from several debilitating surgeries. And yes, it has kept me busy, since every Wednesday comes often, but it has become one of the most rewarding experiences of my life. I'm learning the Book of Mormon as never before on many levels. The most surprising awareness has come as the Book of Mormon people have become real.

Though the Book of Mormon is basically a history and makes no attempt to create an emotional attachment or give details about individuals' lives, at times, I have felt I was present and experiencing life with them. For example, in Alma 5, I felt Alma was looking at me as he was giving his talk. I felt his sense of urgency. I felt the warnings. I thought, "He's asking so many questions." I wanted a mirror to see the countenance on my face. I desperately wanted to be in the fold of the Good Shepherd. I marveled at Alma's articulate way of expressing difficult concepts and felt his Spirit-filled words.

I am surprised over and over as I *feel* with Book of Mormon people. Let me share a few additional examples:

- When Lehi and Sariah were leaving Jerusalem, I wanted to help Sariah pack. I marveled as she was willing to leave almost all their earthly possessions, knowing they would not be returning.
- I felt panic when Zoram and Nephi were walking towards his brothers, who were hiding outside the walls of Jerusalem. I breathed a sigh of relief when Zoram made an oath to go with Nephi and stay with him.
- I felt Lehi's surprise when he saw the Liahona outside his tent door.
- I felt the faith and hope that carried Lehi through the Arabian Desert. I felt his fatherly love for Laman and Lemuel when he gave them his

last earthly blessing and commanded, "Arise from the dust, my sons, and be men" (2 Nephi 1:21).

- I smiled when Abinadi entered the city in disguise and then said, "I am Abinadi."
- When Zeezrom began to ask questions that showed his heart was softening, I felt hope, as though I knew him as a friend.
- I felt squeamish when Zerahemnah lost his scalp.
- When Amalickiah poisoned Lehonti by degrees, I felt infuriated and betrayed.
- I saw myself in Abish when she tried to create a situation in which her people could experience a miracle. When the scene started to look more like chaos than a miracle, I felt her anxiety and fear. When she reached out and lifted the queen by her hand, I admired her courage and felt the miracle of the moment.
- I marveled at Alma's courage to escape from King Noah's wrath. I love how he baptized Helam and himself in the Waters of Mormon.
- I smiled when an angel appeared to Alma outside of Ammonihah and told him that he was the same angel who had appeared to him before.
- I mourned with Alma, son of Alma, when Corianton left his mission for a harlot and rejoiced when Corianton repented and returned to missionary work.
- I worried about Corianton's safety when he went with Hagoth on a ship to who knows where. I wondered if he would become a prophet in the new land.
- I marveled at how quickly Amulek understood the finer points of the gospel.
- I bounced around in one of the eight Jaredite barges for a year as we crossed an angry ocean, being continuously blown by winds towards the promised land.
- I smiled when the valiant, courageous, wise, and righteous Captain Moroni had a moment of impatience that included accusations and name-calling in his letter to Pahoran, the chief judge.
- I admired the courage of the prophets in the time of King Shule as they were harassed and persecuted. I likewise admired the courage of King Shule when he sent a proclamation throughout the land declaring a law to protect the prophets. I was amazed when, because the prophets were free to preach, the people repented and there was no more war in the days of Shule the king.

- I lay in fear as the earth heaved and convulsed at the death of Jesus Christ. I was there when the voice of God, the Eternal Father, acknowledged His Beloved Son. I heard another voice, the voice of Jesus Christ, explain which cities were destroyed and why. I was at the Bountiful temple with about twenty-five hundred other survivors when the resurrected Jesus Christ appeared.

- After I finished the book of Jarom, I thought of him as a real person and imagined how I would meet him in the future. I wrote down some thoughts that became a poem of sorts.

Jarom

I'm too tired to read tonight.
"Oh, just one chapter," says a still small voice.
Well, all right, where am I?
Remembering, I turn crinkly pages past Enos
To another one-chapter book—the Book of Jarom.
Obeying his father's command, Jarom writes for unborn readers.
But the plates are small,
Only bits of history, genealogy, and testimony fit.
Righteous Nephites keep Moses' law,
Understand salvation's plan
Believe in Christ as though He'd come.
Prophets preach revealed words
To the stiff of neck and hard of heart.
Lamanites war, murder, drink beasts' blood.
Two hundred years have passed.
A familiar cycle recycles—
Righteous prosper, pride increases, war.
Prophets preach, pride decreases, peace.
Son Omni now to keep.
Pausing, the leather still between my hands,
a celestial panorama, unbidden,
lifts back the curtains of my mind.
I see glistening, white-robed beings conversing.
"Come," my escort beckons.
Meekly following with naked feet on marbled floor,
we approach a group conversing.
Gesturing towards a heavenly man,

> my escort says, after calling me by name,
> "I would like you to meet Jarom."
> Looking up to meet his gentle eyes, I whisper,
> "I've read your book."

The people of the Book of Mormon are that real to me, as real as my parents and grandparents who have passed on. President Joseph F. Smith saw them. "All these and many more, even the prophets who dwelt among the Nephites and testified of the coming of the Son of God, mingled in the vast assembly and waited for their deliverance" (Doctrine and Covenants 138:49). Our Book of Mormon heroes and friends live nearby, just on the other side of the veil.

Evidence 21
Time Keepers

ANOTHER REMARKABLE FEATURE OF THE Book of Mormon is that it keeps internal calendars. As we know, Joseph dictated the information on the gold plates to scribes one time through, in sixty-five working days without referencing notes, rewriting drafts, reviewing previous text, or using research materials in sixty-five working days. If that is not impossible enough, on the first page, the Book of Mormon boldly asserts that Zedekiah, king of Judah, and Lehi were contemporaries in Jerusalem. From Old Testament chronology, we know that Zedekiah was king from 597 to 587 BC.

In the next few pages, the first countdown is mentioned that the Messiah will come in 600 years. Thus, the counting starts to the birth of Jesus Christ: "Six hundred years since my father left Jerusalem" (see 1 Nephi 10:4, 1 Nephi 19:8, 2 Nephi 25:19). It is simply impossible that Joseph could have kept such a chronology. Here are a few examples:

- Thirty years had passed away from the time we left Jerusalem. (2 Nephi 5:28)
- Fifty and five years had passed away from the time that Lehi left Jerusalem. (Jacob 1:1)
- An hundred and seventy and nine years had passed away from the time that our father Lehi left Jerusalem. (Enos 1:25)
- Mosiah began to reign in his father's stead . . . in the thirtieth year of his age, making in the whole, about four hundred and seventy-six years from the time that Lehi left Jerusalem. (Mosiah 6:4)
- Mosiah died . . . in the thirty and third year of his reign, being sixty and three years old; making in the whole, five hundred and nine years from the time Lehi left Jerusalem. (Mosiah 29:46)
- The ninety and first year had passed away and it was six hundred years from the time that Lehi left Jerusalem. (3 Nephi 1:1)

- And six hundred and nine years had passed away since Lehi left Jerusalem. (3 Nephi 2:6)

From these examples, you see the countdown through the different books from Nephi to Jacob to Enos to Mosiah to Alma to 3 Nephi.

To further complicate the internal calendar of the Book of Mormon, King Mosiah institutes a new form of government, switching from a monarchy to a system of judges that starts a counting up. The first year of the reign of the judges begins in Alma 1. The phrase "reign of the judges" is found one hundred times in the Book of Mormon. The last "reign of the judges" is in the ninetieth year in Helaman 16:24. Figure the complexity of counting down to the birth of Jesus Christ and counting up for the years of the reigns of the judges.

The third counting starts after the coming of Christ.

- In the thirty and fourth year, in the first month, on the fourth day of the month, there arose a great storm, such an one as never had been known in all the land. (3 Nephi 8:5)
- Until an hundred and ten years had passed away; and the first generation from Christ had passed away, and there was no contention in all the land. (4 Nephi 1:18)
- And thus did two hundred and fifty years pass away, and also two hundred and sixty years. (4 Nephi 1:41)
- All the sacred records [were kept] —even until the three hundred and twentieth year from the coming of Christ. (4 Nephi 1:48)
- Behold, four hundred years have passed away since the coming of our Lord and Savior. (Mormon 8:6)

Three complicated timelines intertwined and maintained with accuracy for one thousand years of Nephite/Lamanite history! More than impossible without divine oversight and direction.

All this and more in 65 working days.

Evidence 22
Did Joseph Smith Plagiarize
the Sermon on the Mount?

SOME WHO THINK JOSEPH SMITH wrote the Book of Mormon use the Sermon at the Temple in 3 Nephi 12–18 as evidence of plagiarism. They claim these chapters are too similar to the Sermon on the Mount in Matthew 5–7.

Three points:

1. It is logical that the teachings of Jesus would be similar wherever He spoke, which does not indicate plagiarism but revealed truth.

2. Since the King James Version of the Bible was familiar to Joseph, it seems logical that the words he read aloud to his scribes from the Urim and Thummim would be in scriptural language with which he was familiar.

3. Though very similar, the two sermons have significant differences. Before doing a verse-by-verse comparison, I would like to call Emma Smith as a witness.

Emma was one of Joseph's scribes as he dictated the text of the Book of Mormon. In an interview with her son Joseph Smith III, she testified of how the text of the Book of Mormon came to be. When the interview took place, it had been thirty-five years since Carthage, and she was married to Lewis Bidamon. The date of the interview is early 1879. She passed away April 30, 1879. The transcript was published in the *Saints Herald*, October 1, 1879.

Joseph III: What of the truth of Mormonism?

Emma: I know Mormonism to be the truth; and believe the Church to have been established by divine direction. I have complete faith in it. In writing for your father, I frequently wrote day after day, often sitting at the table close by him, he sitting with his face buried in his hat, with the stone in it, and dictating hour after hour with nothing between us.

Joseph III: Had he not a book or manuscript from which he read, or dictated to you?

Emma: He had neither manuscript nor book to read from.

Joseph III: Could he not have had, and you not know it?

Emma: If he had had anything of the kind, he could not have concealed it from me.

Thank you, Emma and Joseph Smith III. Now let's set the stage for the two sermons.

Where did the sermons take place?

THE SERMON ON THE MOUNT took place on a hillside overlooking the Sea of Galilee.

THE SERMON AT THE TEMPLE took place at or near the temple in Bountiful in ancient America. The temple likely resembled Solomon's temple, following the pattern established. "And I, Nephi, did build a temple; and I did construct it after the manner of the temple of Solomon save it were not built of so many precious things; for they were not to be found upon the land, wherefore, it could not be built like unto Solomon's temple. But the manner of the construction was like unto the temple of Solomon; and the workmanship thereof was exceedingly fine" (2 Nephi 5:16).

How many people attended the sermons?

SERMON ON THE MOUNT: more than 5,000
SERMON AT THE TEMPLE: about 2,500

Who attended the sermons?

SERMON ON THE MOUNT: Jews, Gentiles, believers, non-believers, friends, and foes

SERMON AT THE TEMPLE: In Bountiful, Jesus spoke to a more prepared and spiritual audience. Many wicked Nephites and Lamanites had died in the natural disasters, and the survivors had been significantly humbled by the devastation. Most importantly, the previous day, at the Savior's invitation, the people gathered at the temple had felt the nail prints in his hands and feet and had thrust their hands in his side. The people were ready to receive higher doctrine. Their testimonies were sure. They knew.

Why are the verse numbers the same in Matthew 5 and 3 Nephi 12?
The original manuscripts for both accounts had no chapters or verses. These were added later. According to Wikipedia, in the early thirteenth century, Archbishop Stephen Langton devised the numbering system still used in the Bible today. The Book of Mormon numbering system was created in 1879 by Elder Orson Pratt, which he patterned after the King James Bible for easier reference. (See https://www.churchofjesuschrist.org/study/manual/about-the-scriptures/history?lang=eng#title19.)

Differences in Matthew 5:3 and 3 Nephi 12:3
    BIBLE: "Blessed are the poor in spirit: for theirs is the kingdom of heaven."
    BOOK OF MORMON: "Yea, blessed are the poor in spirit who come unto me, for theirs is the kingdom of heaven."
    The Nephite version is specific: You are poor in spirit if you come unto me.

Differences in Matthew 5:6 and 3 Nephi 12:6
    BIBLE: "Blessed are they which do hunger and thirst after righteousness: for they shall be filled."
    BOOK OF MORMON: "And blessed are all they who do hunger and thirst after righteousness, for they shall be filled with the Holy Ghost."
    The people assembled on the hillside in Galilee didn't know with what they would be filled. The Nephites were promised the Holy Ghost.

Differences in Matthew 5:10 and 3 Nephi 12:10
    BIBLE: "Blessed are they which are persecuted for righteousness' sake: for theirs is the kingdom of heaven."
    BOOK OF MORMON: "And blessed are all they who are persecuted for my name's sake, for theirs is the kingdom of heaven."
    The two references would be more similar if the New Testament version capitalized *Righteousness*, to specify for Jesus's sake.

Differences in Matthew 5:14, 16 and 3 Nephi 12:14, 16
    BIBLE: "Ye are the light of the world. A city that is set on an hill cannot be hid. . . . Let your light so shine before men, that they may see your good works, and glorify your Father which is in heaven."
    BOOK OF MORMON: "Verily, verily, I say unto you, I give unto you to be the light of this people. A city that is set on a hill cannot be hid. . . . Therefore let your light so shine before this people, that they may see your good works and glorify your Father who is in heaven."

Jesus Christ, *the* Light of the World, promised *light* to the Nephites. His pronouncement, "I give unto you" is an endowment of power. "This people" may have a double meaning: the people within your sphere of influence and people of the house of Israel.

Differences in Matthew 5:19 and 3 Nephi 12:19

BIBLE: "Whosoever therefore shall break one of these least commandments, and shall teach men so, he shall be called the least in the kingdom of heaven: but whosoever shall do and teach them, the same shall be called great in the kingdom of heaven."

BOOK OF MORMON: "And behold, I have given you the law and the commandments of my Father, that ye shall believe in me, and that ye shall repent of your sins, and come unto me with a broken heart and a contrite spirit. Behold, ye have the commandments before you, and the law is fulfilled."

Jesus taught the Nephites that the law and the commandments are His Father's. Also, He used "a broken heart and a contrite spirit," which is found seven times in all scripture: six times in the Book of Mormon and one time in the Doctrine and Covenants 59:8.

Differences in Matthew 5:20 and 3 Nephi 12:20

BIBLE: "For I say unto you, that except your righteousness shall exceed the righteousness of the scribes and Pharisees, ye shall in no case enter into the kingdom of heaven." (No more is required of you except that you be better than the scribes and Pharisees.)

BOOK OF MORMON: "Therefore come unto me and be ye saved; for verily I say unto you, that except ye shall keep my commandments, which I have commanded you at this time, ye shall in no case enter into the kingdom of heaven."

Jesus set requirements above and beyond the "righteousness" of the scribes and Pharisees. The command is personal. Keep the commandments and come unto Jesus.

Differences in Matthew 5:21 and 3 Nephi 12:21

BIBLE: "Ye have heard that it was said by them of old time" is one of six examples in which Jesus referred to hearing the word of God (Matthew 5:21, 27, 31, 33, 38, 43).

BOOK OF MORMON: "Ye have heard that it hath been said by them of old time, and it is also written before you." Jesus referred to reading the word of God in 3 Nephi 12:21, 27, 33, 38, 43. (The people of Jerusalem at this time must have *heard* more than they *read*.)

Differences in Matthew 5:22 and 3 Nephi 12:22

BIBLE: "But I say unto you, That whosoever is angry with his brother without a cause shall be in danger of the judgment."

BOOK OF MORMON: "But I say unto you, that whosoever is angry with his brother shall be in danger of his judgment."

"Without a cause" is missing in the Nephite account. "Without a cause" is also not in the oldest known manuscript of the Bible. "Jerome, a fourth-century Catholic priest, scholar, and translator of the Latin Vulgate Bible, stated: 'In some codices [manuscripts] "without cause" is added; however in the authentic codices the statement is unqualified and anger is completely forbidden, for if we are commanded to pray for those who persecute us, every occasion for anger is eliminated. "Without cause" then should be deleted, since the anger of man does not work the justice of God'" (https://rsc.byu.edu/how-new-testament-came-be/adding-taking-away-without-cause-matthew-522). We believe the Bible to be the word of God as far as it is translated correctly. (Articles of Faith 1:8).

Differences in Matthew 5:26 and 3 Nephi 12:26

BIBLE: "Verily I say unto thee, Thou shalt by no means come out thence, till thou hast paid the uttermost farthing." (The coinage used in Palestine.)

BOOK OF MORMON: "Verily, verily, I say unto thee, thou shalt by no means come out thence until thou hast paid the uttermost senine." (A weight of gold or silver used by the Nephites.)

Differences in Matthew 5:29–30 and 3 Nephi 12:29–30

BIBLE: "And if thy right eye offend thee, pluck it out, and cast it from thee: for it is profitable for thee that one of thy members should perish, and not that thy whole body should be cast into hell. And if thy right hand offend thee, cut it off, and cast it from thee: for it is profitable for thee that one of thy members should perish, and not that thy whole body should be cast into hell."

BOOK OF MORMON: "Behold, I give unto you a commandment, that ye suffer none of these things to enter into your heart; For it is better that ye should deny yourselves of these things, wherein ye will take up your cross, than that ye should be cast into hell." (No bodily harm is indicated.)

Differences in Matthew 5:46–47 and 3 Nephi 12:46–47

BIBLE: "For if ye love them which love you, what reward have ye? Do not even the publicans the same? And if ye salute your brethren only, what do ye more than others? Do not even the publicans so?

BOOK OF MORMON: "Therefore those things which were of old time, which were under the law, in me are all fulfilled. Old things are done away, and all things have become new."

Differences in Matthew 5 and 3 Nephi 12:
BIBLE: "Come unto me" is found 0 times in this chapter.
BOOK OF MORMON: "Come unto me" is found 6 times in this chapter:
- Yea, blessed are the poor in spirit who *come unto me*, for theirs is the kingdom of heaven. (v. 3)
- Ye shall repent of your sins, and *come unto me* with a broken heart and a contrite spirit. (v. 19)
- Therefore *come unto me* and be ye saved. (v. 20)
- Therefore, if ye shall *come unto me*, or shall desire to *come unto me*, and rememberest that thy brother hath aught against thee . . . (v. 23)
- Go thy way unto thy brother, and first be reconciled to thy brother, and then *come unto me* with full purpose of heart, and I will receive you. (v. 24)

Differences in Parables in the Sermon on the Mount and Sermon at the Temple
BIBLE: Jesus taught the parables of the Sower (Matthew 13:1–23); the wheat and the tares (Matthew 13:24–30, 36–43); the mustard seed and the hidden leaven (Matthew 13:31–33); the hidden treasure and the pearl of great price (Matthew 13:44–46); and the gospel net (Matthew 13:47–50).

BOOK OF MORMON: There no parables in the Sermon at the Temple in chapter 13. Why? Jesus's disciples in Palestine asked Him why He spoke in parables. Jesus answered: I teach them "in parables: because they seeing see not; and hearing they hear not, neither do they understand" (Matthew 13:13). Jesus could speak more openly and clearly to the Nephites because of their spiritual preparation. Also, the parables Jesus taught in Palestine applied to the culture of that land.

No plagiarism here. Rather the fulfillment of Ezekiel's prophecy that the stick of Judah—the Bible—and the stick of Ephraim—The Book of Mormon—will "join . . . one to another into one stick; and they shall become one in thine hand" (Ezekiel 37:16–17).

Postlude

THIS IS THE END NOT because there is nothing more to write about the resurrection of gold plates buried in a stone box on the side of a hill in upstate New York in sixty-five days but because there is too much more. Joseph Smith gave the Book of Mormon to the world through the gift, power, and mercy of God.

The purpose of this book is to help you enjoy the assembled evidences to motivate you to find others on your own. Every evidence builds on every other evidence; every testimony builds on every other testimony. Every prophet in the Book of Mormon builds on every other prophet's testimony; and added to those are the testimonies of the latter-day prophets. I leave it to them, the prophets, seers, and revelators, to have the last word:

Joseph Smith: "The Book of Mormon [is] the most correct of any book on earth, and the keystone of our religion, and a man [will] get nearer to God by abiding by its precepts, than by any other book" (*Teachings of the Prophet Joseph Smith*, comp. Joseph Fielding Smith [Salt Lake City: Deseret Book, 1976], 194).

Brigham Young: "The Book of Mormon . . . declares that the Bible is true, and it proves it; and the two prove each other true" (https://www.churchofjesuschrist.org/study/manual/teachings-brigham-young/chapter-17?lang=eng).

John Taylor: "To seal the testimony of this book and the Book of Mormon, we announce the martyrdom of Joseph Smith the Prophet, and Hyrum Smith the Patriarch" (Doctrine and Covenants 135:1).

Wilford Woodruff: "These principles were rivetted upon my mind from the perusal of the Old and New Testament, with fervent prayer that the Lord would show me what was right and wrong, and lead me in the path of salvation. We read the Book of Mormon, and I received a testimony that it was true" (https://www.fairlatterdaysaints.org/fair-come-follow-me-2023/preparing-your-family-for-a-lifetime-on-the-covenant-path/asking-big-questions-how-can-i-gain-a-testimony-of-the-book-of-mormon).

Lorenzo Snow: "It was a knowledge far beyond that of belief or opinion. I knew that God had sent His angels and restored the fullness of the Gospel as taught in ancient times; that He sent angels to authorize Joseph Smith, and gave him authority to administer in the ordinances of the Gospel, and to promise the Holy Ghost to all who would be obedient" (https://www.ldsscriptureteachings.org/2017/01/lorenzo-snows-witness).

Joseph F. Smith: "Here, then, are two witnesses—the Bible and the Book of Mormon, both bearing record of the same truth, that Jesus was the Christ, that he died and lives again, having burst the bands of death and triumphed over the grave" (https://www.churchofjesuschrist.org/study/manual/teachings-joseph-f-smith/chapter-23?lang=eng).

Heber J. Grant: "The Book of Mormon is the great, the grand, the most wonderful missionary that we have" (https://www.thechurchnews.com/1988/1/2/23264417/latter-day-prophets-have-emphasized-books-worth).

George Albert Smith: "It fills my heart with joy to know that every man who will read [the Book of Mormon] prayerfully, every man who will desire to know whether it be of God or not has the promise, not of Joseph Smith or any living being, but the promise of our Heavenly Father that they shall know of a surety that it is of God" (https://www.churchofjesuschrist.org/study/ensign/2011/10/the-book-of-mormon-keystone-of-our-religion?lang=eng).

David O. McKay: "The Book of Mormon itself is the best memorial to the claim of the vision of the Prophet Joseph Smith" (https://www.thechurchnews.com/1988/1/2/23264417/latter-day-prophets-have-emphasized-books-worth).

Joseph Fielding Smith: "It seems to me that any member of this Church would never be satisfied until he or she had read the Book of Mormon time and time again and thoroughly considered it so that he or she could bear witness that it is in very deed a record with the inspiration of the Almighty upon it" (https://www.churchofjesuschrist.org/study/manual/teachings-of-presidents-of-the-church-joseph-fielding-smith/chapter-9-witnesses-of-the-book-of-mormon?lang=eng).

Harold B. Lee: "Joseph Smith could not have established this church. He could not have brought forth the work of the Lord, the Book of Mormon. They may scoff at the Prophet Joseph Smith as a man. They may question how this church began, but here the thing stands as a monument—the Book of Mormon itself. Joseph, the man, could not have done this, but Joseph, actuated by the power of Almighty God, could and did perform the miraculous service of bringing forth the kingdom out of obscurity in the restored gospel of Jesus Christ" (https://www.churchofjesuschrist.org/study/manual/teachings-harold-b-lee/chapter-8?lang=eng).

Spencer W. Kimball: "I now add my personal and solemn testimony that God, the Eternal Father, and the risen Lord, Jesus Christ, appeared to the boy Joseph Smith. I testify that the Book of Mormon is a translation of an ancient record of nations who once lived in [the] western hemisphere, where they prospered and became mighty when they kept the commandments of God, but who were largely destroyed through terrible civil wars when they forgot God" (https://www.churchofjesuschrist.org/study/manual/teachings-spencer-w-kimball/chapter-7?lang=eng).

Ezra Taft Benson: "The Book of Mormon is the instrument that God designed to 'sweep the earth as with a flood, to gather out [His] elect'" (https://www.churchofjesuschrist.org/study/ensign/2005/10/flooding-the-earth-with-the-book-of-mormon?lang=eng).

Howard W. Hunter: "I am grateful that in addition to the Old and New Testaments, the Lord, through prophets of The Church of Jesus Christ of Latter-day Saints, has added other revealed scripture as additional witnesses for Christ—the Book of Mormon, the Doctrine and Covenants, and the Pearl of Great Price—all of which I know to be the word of God. These bear witness that Jesus is the Christ, the Son of the living God" (https://www.churchofjesuschrist.org/study/manual/teachings-of-presidents-of-the-church-howard-w-hunter/chapter-10-the-scriptures-the-most-profitable-of-all-study?lang=eng).

Gordon B. Hinckley: "I have read the Book of Mormon, again and again. I know that [Joseph] did not write it out of his own capacity. I know that he was a translator who by the gift and power of God brought forth this great testament of the New World. I know that it is true, that it is powerful, that it is a witness to the nations of the Divine Redeemer of mankind, the Living Son of the Living God" (https://rsc.byu.edu/joseph-smith-prophet-man/one-who-loves-prophet).

Thomas S. Monson: "The importance of having a firm and sure testimony of the Book of Mormon cannot be overstated" (https://www.churchof jesuschrist.org/study/general-conference/2017/04/the-power-of-the-book-of-mormon?lang=eng).

Russell M. Nelson: "My dear brothers and sisters, I promise that as you prayerfully study the Book of Mormon every day, you will make better decisions—every day" (https://www.churchofjesuschrist.org/inspiration/president-nelson-promises-scripture-power?lang=eng).

About the Author

MARILYNNE TODD LINFORD HAS A passion for history—the Reformation, Colonial American, the Restoration of The Church of Jesus Christ of Latter-day Saints. Writing family histories is another passion because she knows those who *write* history *make* history. Only those things that are recorded are remembered. She graduated from the University of Utah in history and English. She was a member of the Church Materials Evaluation Committee for eleven years, a docent in the Church History Museum for twenty years, and a columnist for *Meridian Magazine* for four years. For the past two years, she has taught a weekly Book of Mormon class on Zoom. She has written thirteen books and many chapters in anthologies and articles in magazines. Her most beautiful moments come when she is with any combination of family at home, playing word games or piano duets, visiting a Church or national historic site, walking on warm sandy beaches, hiking the red rock canyons of Southern Utah, or picnicking in Mill Creek Canyon near her home. As the oldest of eight, mother of eight, mother-in-law of eight, grandmother of twenty-nine, and great-grandmother of nine, she has many opportunities to experience love and life. She feels blessed to have been continually educated as she and Richard have read together nearly every day since they were married fifty-six years ago. She survived breast cancer twice, in 1996 and 2015, and most recently, broke ten vertebrae. If she had to list her premiere delight in life, right after doing anything family, it would be teaching and writing about the Book of Mormon.